God Appointments™

Everything I Never Knew I Needed

Sincerely,
Bobbie Suzette

PRESS

Jesus called a little child to him, and placed the child among them. And he said: "Truly I tell you, unless you change and become like little children, you will never enter the kingdom of heaven."
Matthew 18:2-3

The motive behind God Appointments is to learn how to be like little children...completely dependent on God.

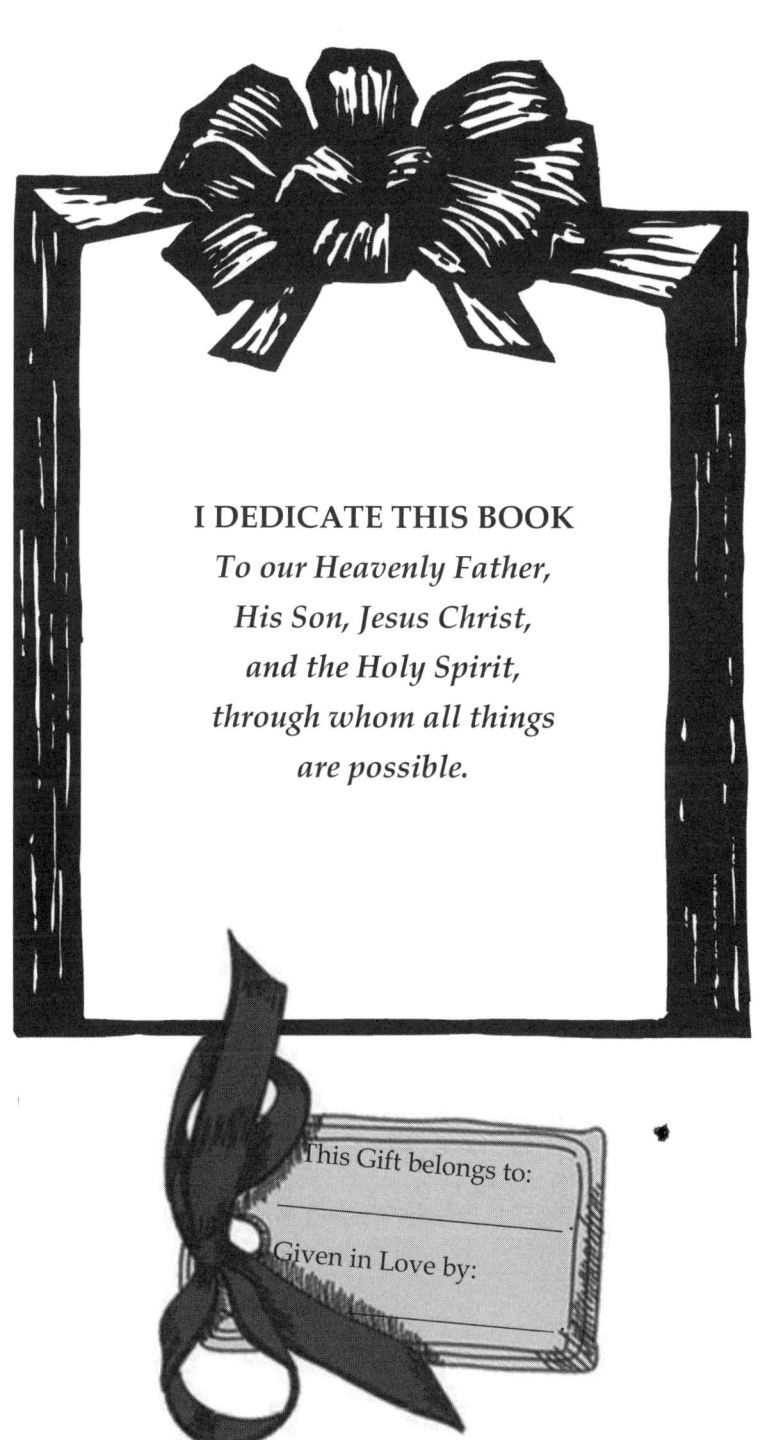

I DEDICATE THIS BOOK

To our Heavenly Father,
His Son, Jesus Christ,
and the Holy Spirit,
through whom all things
are possible.

This Gift belongs to:

_____

Given in Love by:

_____

Image Statement

God Appointments is not just a book with a few interesting stories written by some person who lives on the edge. Rather, it is a book about the desire written into the code of each of us to become a more **accurate** reflection of God's image, thereby bringing Him pleasure and us fulfillment as we recognize that our lives serve a grander purpose.

God Appointments is about going into God's world and living out the original "image statement." *Missions* was never meant to be the goal and intent of mankind or the church. *Worship* is the true goal of the Christian life — the kind of worship that comes when we **accurately** reflect God's image in the world. This kind of worship cannot be confined to or fulfilled in just an hour or so on Sunday.

Missions exist only because there are places in the world where this kind of worship does not exist. With this idea in mind, Jesus made His famous Great Commission statement, recorded in the Book of Matthew. But this is actually a *recommission* of God's original "Go into all earth and bear my image" statement in Genesis. When Adam failed to do this, God sent the second "Adam" — Jesus — to complete the picture and make God's image known. Jesus said, "If you have seen me, you have seen the Father."

So wherever in this world there is not an **accurate** image or reflection of God and His intention, we must go and bear His image through holistic love and discipleship. This is why we were created. This is what brings God pleasure.

As you read God Appointments, may you understand how you can more fully reflect the image of Jesus in your world.

Pastor Douglas Ehrgott
Global Team Builder, Horizon International

Nothing New

There is **nothing new** about *God Appointments*. In fact, there is something very old about this book, because it represents awareness of what has been and what always will be. For thousands of years, the Bible has been our undeniable source and guide for God's will for our lives. Written over the course of 1,500 years by 40 different authors in three languages throughout three continents with no contradictions is a miracle in itself. And that's not to mention the 191 (or more) predictions in the Old Testament that are fulfilled in the New Testament. For this number of predictions to be confirmed is a one-in-a-trillion chance by any scientific standard. There is no worldly explanation. It only is possible if it is the true Word of God.

The Old Testament is the New Testament concealed, and the New Testament is the Old Testament revealed.

People find many reasons not to accept Jesus and the Holy Spirit. Some common reasons are religious confusion, suffering, negative exposure, private agendas and all other deceptions this world brings. This also is **nothing new**.

But God's people have had enough of satan's schemes through false religion and manmade rules. It's time to uncover the meaning of God's word to *all* people and to reveal the most misunderstood truth.

One evening I was sitting in bed working on this book when my daughter Robbie Sue called. After reading the *God*

Appointments manuscript, she was excited because she'd found scripture regarding the Spirit and had understood the true meaning for the first time. She was so sweet when she said, "Mom, this stuff is *real.*"

I got my Bible and looked up the scripture she'd given me. As I read the second chapter of 1 Corinthians, I wept. I had read this chapter before, but now it had **new meaning**. It was a hidden treasure uncovered by God for me.

God Appointments is nothing more than a tool to help us uncover what you and I have been given in Christ. The Bible is the only source we will ever need (1 John 2:26–27). Other books, including this one, are helpful—but always remember the Bible is living and is the only book that can connect us with God through Jesus and give us understanding of the Holy Spirit. I invite you to read the scripture listed below *before and after* you read this book. After you read *God Appointments*, I pray this scripture will be alive in your heart and this new **understanding** will give you everything you never knew you needed.

1 Corinthians 2 (NIV)
Inspired through the apostle Paul

*When I came to you, brothers, I did not come with eloquence or superior wisdom as I proclaimed to you the testimony about God. For I resolved to **know nothing** while I was with you except Jesus Christ and him crucified. I came to you in **weakness** and **fear**, and with much **trembling**. My message and my preaching were not with wise and persuasive words, but with a demonstration of the **Spirit's power**, so that your faith might not rest on men's wisdom, but on **God's power**.*

*We do, however, speak a message of wisdom among the mature, but **not** the wisdom of this age or of the rulers of this age, who are coming to **nothing**. No, we speak of **God's secret wisdom,** a wisdom that has **been hidden** and that **God destined for our glory before time began**. None of the rulers of this age understood it, for if they* had, they would **not** have crucified the Lord of glory. However, as it is written:

> **"No eye has seen,**
> **no ear has heard,**
> **no mind has conceived**
> what **God has prepared** for those who love him"
> — but God has **revealed** it to us by **his Spirit.**

The Spirit searches all things, even the deep things of God. For who among men knows the thoughts of a man except the man's **spirit within him**? In the same way no one knows the thoughts of God except the **Spirit of God**. We have not received the spirit of the world but the **Spirit who is from God**, that we may **understand** what God has freely given us. This is what we speak, not in words taught us by human wisdom but in words **taught by the Spirit,** expressing spiritual truths in spiritual words. The man without the Spirit **does not accept** the things that come from the **Spirit of God**, for they are foolishness to him, and he cannot understand them, because they are **spiritually discerned**. The spiritual man makes judgments about all things, but he himself is not subject to any man's judgment:

> **"For who has known the mind of the Lord**
> **that he may instruct him?" But we have the mind of Christ.**

Favor

For you are our glory and strength,
and by your favor you exalt our horn.
Psalm 89:17

There are not enough pages to thank all the people who've made a difference in my life. To each of you I am forever grateful. The creation of *God Appointments* was perfectly positioned for a **moment** in time. I believe God chose certain people to release this message. We aren't more important; we were just available for a time such as this.

I am humbled to thank each of you in the name of Jesus for being His hands and feet—for encouraging me when I had fear, for praying when I had doubt and for carrying me when I was too tired to walk on my own. This **favor** is important because it is yours to keep. My words will come and go, but the gift of God's favor will be with you for a lifetime.

To my husband, **Brian Lincoln**—Thank you for allowing me to grow into a woman God could use. From my first mission trip to writing this book, you have never complained. Without your patience and support, I could not have taken the time to release the Holy Spirit to love and care for God's people. Thank you for loving our wild and crazy family just as we are. You are **faithful**!

To my daughters, **Billie LeSure** and **Robbie Webster**— God gave me much more than I could ever deserve when he gave me you two. One of my greatest joys is watching you love and support each other. You have been my teachers and a picture of how Jesus loves. You both are the kind of wives, mothers and daughters I always wanted to be. What amazes me most is even as little girls you were **willing** to share me with my God Appointments, even when you felt that you were last on my list. Now you know the love you received was far greater because I *first* loved Jesus. Your example continues to grow in me!

To my parents, **La Verne** and **Bonnie De Young**—I am grateful I didn't grow up in a perfect family. You both taught me that our love for each other means more than any differences this world can bring. Dad, though you are not with me here on earth, your love continues to guide my steps. You showed me how to love God's people and never, never, never give up. Mom, you taught me that I'm always enough for God, because I was always enough for you. I still count on you to tell me, "Bobbie Sue, it will be okay." Together you **believed** in me when I didn't believe in myself. Forever and always!

To my sister, **Lisa Swims**—Sissy, you made me realize this book was truly from God and gave me courage to take one more step. Your love for Jesus overflowed to me, and with each conversation you gave me the belief that I could write. Through your faith, I knew God was working because you know who I am without Him. God allowed me to watch you become a **new creation** in Christ, and then I experienced the Holy Spirit through you. Your wisdom and revelation brought me the messages needed to deliver *God Appointments*. I believe!

To my dear friend, **Theresa Anderson**—You have taken each breath of this journey with me. Not one day went by without a nudge to inspire me to give more and be more for God. You have lived every word on these pages, and you did it willingly. You never take credit and yet there would be no book without your **sacrifice**. You have been behind the scenes coaching and pushing me to deliver a gift worthy of God's Kingdom. I made a mess, and you cleaned it up. You once told me that God put you in my life because He had a job for you. Thanks for the overtime and 24-hour shifts. Sisters in Christ!

To my kindergarten buddy, **Diane Keelan**—Thank you for being a strong influence in my life and keeping me under your wing until I could fly. We have traveled many roads together, and in God's mercy we found the one that led us to the Holy Spirit. Watching you transform into a woman who depends on God is a highlight in my life. You've never been afraid to step out; the difference today is that you **step out** in faith for the Lord. You have respected God's timing for God Appointments and allowed Him to open the doors. I notice!

To my spiritual mentor, **Pastor Douglas J Ehrgott**—As you read this book I hope God reveals the **influence** you have in my life. The pages are filled with your teachings and favorite sayings. I have notes on each of your devotions from Brazil to Africa, not to mention the church services in between. I've often thought this book should have been written by you, and in many ways it was. Your greatest lesson is how you thank  God with your life by loving and caring for the orphans of this world. God gave me time to write so you could stay with Him in Africa. The world will have to wait for the book that dwells within your heart. Go well my friend!

To my editor and friend, **Manda Newlin**—You are the "icing on the cake" for God Appointments and a true definition of Hebrews 11:1. I knew what I hoped for and was certain of what I could not do on my own. You came to me in highest regards referred from the best of the best! Only God knew my situation and through the Holy Spirit you were an answer to  prayer. Your **generosity** will be remembered for generations. It matters!

Special thanks to each person who showed up and allowed me to release God's love through the God Appointments in this book and throughout my life.

Preparation

*Jesus said, Peace be with you! As the Father has
sent me, I am sending you.*
John 20:21

Y ou are about to read *God Appointments*. The term "God
Appointments" may be unfamiliar to you, but you'll
soon understand. Simply put, it describes how my friend
Bobbie lives her life. She is a servant of God who is passionate
about letting God love His people through her. Anyone she
meets will be blessed by the interaction, or "appointment."
These appointments are not scheduled, at least not in the
natural sense. She makes herself available, and God sched-
ules the appointments in His time. I have witnessed many
of Bobbie's appointments and have been told, always to no
surprise, of many more. I'm not surprised because I know she
prays to receive appointments every day. To me, each one is
an inspiring opportunity to witness these miracles of love.

Is She for Real?

As you read this book, you may at times think "She is not
real!" or "How could this all be true?" Or maybe you'll think,
"That's good for her, but I'm not like her. I could never have
these God Appointments." Such thoughts wouldn't surprise
me because I've had all of them myself. But I'm writing to
testify that Bobbie is real and every journal that follows is

entirely true. In fact, these stories don't scratch the surface of Bobbie's daily relationship with God.

More important, I'm writing to testify that it is possible for each of us to experience our own God Appointments. They may not be like Bobbie's; they will be our own.

Bobbie often tells me, "You will reach people that I cannot." She is right; I've seen it happen. We are individually made by God, and He uses each of us differently. Please don't think you have to be like Bobbie or even that you want to be. *God made you who you are for a reason.*

Bobbie is a wonderful example of a person who spreads the love of God wherever she goes. But each of us, in our own way, also can love God's people as He directs us. All we have to do is be willing to open our hearts, our spirits, to His direction.

In this book, Bobbie will teach you from her perspective — that is, one of willingness to accept the appointment from God. I can best describe the miracle of these God Appointments through my own experience — my own God Appointment with Bobbie. Like many of Bobbie's appointments, it wasn't scheduled. Had it been, I probably would not have shown up.

Jesus, Bobbie and Me

I was in my office one day. I'd known Bobbie for a few years and we'd developed a cordial vendor-client relationship. I was drawn to her kindness and spirit, but our relationship was rooted in work and business. On top of that, I tend to be guarded about allowing people into my life at a more personal level. On my own, we would never have anything but a casual, professional relationship of mutual respect. But Bobbie, as always, was willing to let God use her to show me His love through her.

This experience occurred several years ago, but I remember it well because it changed my life.

Bobbie's trademark behavior is just stopping by the office. I tease her about how she breezes by somber security guards and melts rigid receptionists. I think her spirit paves the way, and God allows it.

On this day I looked up from a frustrating project to see Bobbie peeking in my doorway. I welcomed her even though I was way too busy to take the time. She brought a peace with her that's so inviting you forget about the stresses of the moment and you want to know what she has.

I don't remember how we got so deep in conversation when we didn't even know each other very well. It probably began with her saying that she knew I was busy so she wanted only to say a quick hello. But God had an appointment for us that was more than a quick hello.

At this time in my life, I was really struggling—a working mother with young kids, juggling my roles as wife, mom and career woman. Technically I was doing it all, but I felt I wasn't doing any of it well. I was going through the motions of life with no emotions. I'd tucked them all neatly, deeply away and got by each day doing what had to be done. But I was missing something significant and meaningful.

Before I knew it, I was sharing deep feelings with Bobbie. Through her peace and God's love, I felt somehow safe enough to be vulnerable. I told her that I knew I was strong and could get through anything on my own. I knew this because I'd already lived through the toughest challenge I'd ever have to face in my life, an experience I rarely shared with anyone. I told Bobbie that when I was a teenager, I'd lost my mother to cancer. If I could get through that—which I did (or thought I did)—I could get through anything. But I didn't stop there. I shared many painful details and circumstances from that time in my life.

Suddenly I was not so tough anymore. With a shaky voice and teary eyes, I spoke and Bobbie listened. At no other time in my life had I told my story in such detail and revealed so much pain. Shaking up my emotions from my numbness would've been a miracle in itself—but before Bobbie left the real miracle arrived: the revelation about God's love.

Before this appointment, I was a believer. I went to church, prayed with my kids, was kind to strangers and all that "good stuff." At some basic level, I trusted God to take care of my needs. But the enormous thing that was missing was that I knew absolutely nothing about God's love for me. Bobbie said something that day about Jesus Christ, God's son that planted a seed. That seed eventually would help me open up the hardness around my heart and let Him in.

She must have said His name — *Jesus* — several times. Every time she said it, I sensed Jesus was something different to her than I had ever allowed Him to be to me. Hearing His name come from her mouth made a difference to me, *a life-changing difference.*

The change in me may not have been immediate, but the seed was planted. Looking back at the growth in my own relationship with Jesus, it makes sense that relationships are not built instantly. They have to grow on love and trust, which I guess is faith. Strong relationships take time. But I'd been hurt enough that I'd decided subconsciously I could protect myself if I never loved deeply again. This is how I had been "getting by" in my life until that day.

I felt the love of Christ through Bobbie, and though it was scary, I was willing to risk being hurt to open my heart and let God love me. It was easy for me to say that I loved God, but I'd avoided letting Him love me.

The Journey

Since then my journey has continued as I seek to find the ultimate peace and love in God through a relationship with Christ. The journey is my life. Some days I feel His presence, and some days I honestly don't. The difference now is that when I don't feel Him, I know He's there anyway. I'm learning to trust.

Some God Appointments are just a moment in our lives that change us, some last for seasons, and some are the beginning of a lifetime friendship where God is the bond that connects two hearts. The gift God gave me on that appointment was a friend in Christ for a lifetime. In each appointment, God fills a different need. In my case, He knew I wouldn't fully understand or trust His love unless I could witness unconditional, sustained love again—the kind of love my mother gave me, but I had grown to believe it didn't exist, not even from God. He sent Bobbie to show me His love for me. And because of her love for Him and her obedience to His appointments, He found His way into my heart.

My friendship with Bobbie has been a blessing I never knew I needed, and now I can't imagine my life without it. How we became friends makes sense only if God is given all the glory. On the surface we don't seem too much alike. Many people want to question what we have in common that creates our bond. Bobbie likes girly things and can wear her hair in a thousand different styles. I don't think I've ever worn a ponytail in my hair or put on a pair of dangly earrings. Bobbie is open and outward in her worship and witness for the Lord, where I am more reflective. (If this makes sense, she is a "Mary" and I am a "Martha.")

In the natural, this friendship might never have happened. I am Catholic and Bobbie is not. That alone might be a cause of conflict in a spiritual friendship. Sadly, divisions even among Christians are common and must grieve God more than anything else we do as the Body of Christ.

The message of our friendship is very simple: We share a love of Christ, and all our conversations are rooted in that love. Our differences don't matter if we focus on what we have in common. We remind each other who we are in Christ whenever one of us needs another nudge.

Our friendship was able to grow because I realized that every time I was with Bobbie, I learned something about Christ and His love. I gravitate to teachers because I love to learn. But I also try to discern the Truth in any lesson. When I hear something that contradicts what I know to be true, I politely move on. I have been blessed to learn from many well-educated and intelligent theologians and Bible scholars, and I'm so thankful for every lesson that helps me to grow closer to Christ.

Bobbie would be the first to tell you that she is not this kind of teacher. But she *is* a teacher in every sense of the word. Her value comes in the simplicity of her message and her motive for teaching: to share what God has revealed to her through her experiences. Bobbie's faith is childlike in the Biblical sense, pure and unquestioning. Today I am learning that this type of faith is required to fully release the power of God's Spirit in each of us. And I believe this faith allows her to see simple truths that others see but don't see, hear but don't hear. I am so thankful that she has accepted God's calling to share what He has revealed to her.

In the Gospel of Matthew, two verses explain very well why Bobbie possesses such revelation about Christ's gift to us—and why we shouldn't miss what she teaches in *God Appointments*.

> *Jesus said…"I give praise to you, Father, Lord of heaven and earth, for although you have hidden these things from the wise and the learned, you have revealed them to the childlike." (Matthew 11:25)*

> *Amen, I say to you, many prophets and righteous people longed to see what you see but did not see it, and to hear what you hear but did not hear it. (Matthew 13:17)*

> *The New American Bible, © 2004 by Oxford University Press, Inc.*

My Prayer for You

As you read this book, I pray that your heart is prepared and open to Bobbie's teaching. At first, you may be challenged by her teaching. I was. But as I walked alongside her and witnessed her obedience to God, I learned that her message was challenging only because it comes in a different package than what I was used to. When I got out of my comfort zone and opened myself up, I could no longer deny that Bobbie has a clear, truthful message for all who want to know Christ and live as His hands and feet on earth. If you put aside your past conditioning, you will be blessed by this book and by the words God gave Bobbie to share with you.

So many people desperately need someone to be bold enough to accept a God Appointment and enter their lives as a channel for His love. I thank God every day that Bobbie accepted the appointment He sent her on that day in my office years ago.

Together we can find the boldness to ask for His appointments — like Bobbie does — and be willing to go wherever He leads us toward another hurting soul who needs God's love. We can spread His love if we *accept* the appointments He sends us and we *receive* the ones He brings us. Bobbie's witness shows me that, one appointment at a time, God can fill all of our needs through one another.

— A friend in Christ, Theresa Anderson

Table of Contents

The Journey

The Journals

Chapter 1

Invitation
Would You Be Willing?

*My son, if you accept my words and store up my
commands with you,
turning your ear to wisdom and applying your
heart to understanding,
and if you call out for insight and cry aloud for understanding,
and if you look for it as for silver and search for it as
for hidden treasure,
then you will understand the fear of the Lord and find
the knowledge of God.
Proverbs 2:1-6*

If you knew you had gold buried in your back yard, **would you be willing** to dig for it? That is the question for each of us. For me, there was a time when digging didn't seem valuable, or maybe I thought nothing was worth digging for. Whatever the reason, I now know timing is important. The struggle comes when the timing is perfect for God, but we cannot hear Him because we are distracted in our lives.

At my first business seminar, my girlfriend Marty told me not to miss any part of the conference. "You never know when the one nugget you came for is going to be released," she said. One nugget can bring Heaven on Earth to our lives.

When I began writing *God Appointments*, I wasn't sure what God wanted from me. I knew it had to be more than the notes I'd made in my journals over the years. Now, I believe He wanted me to share what I didn't know I had.

In the chapter "Open the Gift," God reveals to me the treasure meant for us here on earth. The teaching is simple yet profound, and I believe it's the reason Jesus died. I'd been taught most of this message in nuggets, and I stored them up over time in my spirit. I used to worry that I wouldn't remember them all. Each was a valuable jewel I didn't want to lose. Someone dear to me said, "You will not lose God's words. They are like treasures stored up in your spirit, and God will recall them as needed."

You must know up front, I am not the teacher in this book. Rather, I am the student. I didn't start out knowing how to write a book, and I didn't write by any rules. I simply recalled the treasures God has given me.

I will confess, I have read these pages more than 100 times. Each time I receive something new. Yet at times some parts have been challenging. If you have to put the book down, promise yourself that you'll pick it back up and finish it. If you decide that in advance, the battle is already won. Know that satan does not want you to uncover the language hidden from him by God. With each word in this book, you'll be digging. At completion, the treasure will be yours.

To **uncover** the true meaning of these *God Appointment* journals, you first should read "Open the Gift." This chapter explains why God asked me for what He knew I had—my journals. I started keeping these journals on my early mission trips so I could share the details with my daughters afterward. Later I began writing down the details of past experiences, and I kept new journals to capture appointments as they occurred.

"Open the Gift" also explains why God wants to reveal what most of us don't know we have. In faith Jesus was willing to dig for gold—that is, to *die for God*—because He knew we were the treasure to His Father. The *treasure* for us is what Jesus left behind!

The *treasure* awaits your reply....

— Bobbie Suzette

Chapter 2

It's My Party Guest List "Sinners and Saints"

The party is over and all of the guests have gone home. The garbage needs to go out and the dumpster is full. I ate so much that nothing sounds good. What I really want is to go to sleep and forget about the mess.

Seems like whenever we set out to do something good or celebrate what God has given us, there's always a letdown period or a weakness when the end arrives. Why can't life be a lifelong party? The celebration could be every day from the time we wake up to the moment we fall asleep. Maybe that is what Jesus intended, but the party — that is, the joy of God — is in each of our spirits. But the letdown comes when the enemy covers the spirit with his lies. He is the ultimate party crasher!

The after-party gossip sounds something like this: "What are you saying? God will love us, and we won't lose our place in heaven no matter what? Do you mean we can just do anything we want and live in sin?"

Apostle Paul experienced all of these questions! Romans 6:1 says, *"What shall we say then? Shall we continue in sin, that grace may abound?"* The answer, of course, is Romans 6:2: *"God forbid."*

Paul dealt with the sin questions many times. Yet we continue to feel that forgiveness is impossible. Then, once we learn we are forgiven, our next thought is, *Well, why not sin then?* But it's not really about if we sin, but when we sin. We can agree we all mess up, yet most organizations are not teaching, "You can just go live in sin." Rather, most of us focus on how to conquer sin. And because what we focus on tends to grow, *that* is why sin and false images like addictions, depression and self worship is on the rise. The fact is, we do live in sin — we make mistakes.

Common thinking ties God's love and acceptance to our performance. This message will always produce a works-righteousness believer who feels continually defeated. The Bible doesn't teach that God accepts or rejects us based on our actions; it teaches that our actions can never be good enough. God's Word says He accepts us if *our spirit* is righteous. Righteousness comes through confessing Jesus Christ as our Lord and Savior. Our spirit does not become righteous through our good actions and attitude. When our Spirit takes **first position** in our lives, the overflow of love and goodness naturally shines through and the desire for sin naturally lessens. Goodness is not a task, it is our God-given nature in proper alignment.

Another party rumor: "Are you saying it doesn't matter how we live?" No, that was not taught at the party! Paul gave two more reasons in Romans 6 why a person who loves and accepts Jesus should want to live Holy. First, our new nature desires to please God. Second, we don't want to give the devil access to our mind and body. How we live does not influence our spirit's righteousness, but it greatly affects our life here on earth! The enemy's only goal is to kill and destroy our lives here on earth so we cannot reach out to others. Satan is sure he can break us, but he is risking making us. He takes the risk because most of us don't know what satan knows about the Holy Spirit.

When we are saved through Christ, God changes our nature. We no longer live as a child under the authority of satan. We still mess up, but that behavior is not our first nature anymore. Our spirit has been changed, and we no longer enjoy our bad deeds. Every believer has a built-in desire to fulfill his or her spiritual purpose. We might not always fulfill it, but it is there anyway!

When I read the Bible, I see that God has always focused on *us*—not on our sin. If He hates the sin, perhaps it's only because he hates how sin affects our lives here on earth and how we move away from Him when we go against our spiritual desire to be good. Sin is not a problem for God. That's why satan was thrown out of Heaven in the first place. Satan has never been and will never be a match for God! Satan only has power if we give it to him. The enemy influences our flesh to turn away from God when we think we do things that would disappoint God. Actions could be as simple as not reading our Bible or not showing up to a party when the hosts are expecting us.

In the latter example, shying away from God all starts with the first turn. First, we don't want to face the people who were expecting us. And then we focus on what we did wrong. Next we separate ourselves from that person or people. And if we're not careful, the process repeats itself. The enemy knows that if he gets us by ourselves, he can dominate—and ruin—our lives.

Building our relationship with God takes time on our part. We'll always struggle to develop a friendship with God if we continue to turn away from Him. We must commit to the process of growing, forgiving, communicating, understanding and, most of all, trusting that God loves us **unconditionally.**

Perhaps you have not experienced this kind of unconditional love here on earth, where our "lovability" is typically attached to our behavior. The key is that we do not turn away from God, and in that alone we become stronger in Him than we would've been without the mess-ups.

Every situation is an opportunity for God. Of course, doing the wrong things can really make our lives miserable. We have the choice to turn or not to turn from Jesus. The strength is in not turning away from God or the things here on earth we feel compelled to run from. His strength comes when we meet with His people face to face and heart to heart.

When we try to live by the law, legalism and religious works, our sin (that is, our mess-ups) actually grows stronger. The law in the Old Testament was not given to help us overcome sin. It was to show us that sin had already overcome us! Just knowing that we can communicate with God based on the perfection, holiness and righteousness in our spirit can naturally set us free from so much of our sin. In our flesh we'll never be perfect until we die and our mind and body are dead to us. Yet while we are here on earth, we can grow close to God based on who we are in the spirit. This makes our relationship with Him stable and secure. And so we do not live holy because we have to, but we live holy because we want to. One of my favorite sayings—from Pastor Andrew Wommack—is this: "Just knowing God's love will make us holier accidently than we ever could be through our own efforts."

When we love someone so much, why would we want to do something to hurt that person? I want to please God. The unconditional love He gives me flows out to others beyond what I can even understand in my flesh. When the love of Jesus comes into our lives, love must flow out. It is as natural as breathing. The only reason we inhale (study the Word and Worship the Lord) is to exhale (love and serve God's people). One cannot bring life without the other; actually, it would bring death.

God Appointments happen as we live our lives and walk alongside His people. Sometimes we can get in a habit of inhaling God's Word, as by going to church, and keeping the message all to ourselves. This makes us full of ourselves and leaves us feeling defeated. Our *design* is to love God first by inhaling, and then to love His people as we exhale.

Acts 2:17-18 says, *"In the last days, God says, I will pour out my Spirit on all people. Your sons and daughters will prophesy, your young men will see visions, your old men will dream dreams. Even on my servants, both men and women, I will pour out my Spirit in those days, and they will prophesy."*

This world we live in focuses on all that we don't have: riches, fame, beauty, etc. I believe for many people their focus is obscured because they don't know what we *do have*. God is pouring His Spirit on *all* of us—those of us who believe in Jesus as well as nonbelievers—and we reject that gift because we do not recognize or understand the reason it comes.

Meanwhile the enemy continues to remove the life of the Spirit from our churches. People young and old are searching for the life of His Spirit. They can sense something deep within themselves—a yearning, a desire and the purpose they were created for. Our young people are drawn to the spirits of this world that aren't from God because it's all they know. The dark spirits of this world are available, ready and willing. Young people naturally desire to give their spirit away. God created this desire in us, but I believe His intention is that the mature among us are here to teach, show and train in the way His people—our children—should go.

If we don't know how to communicate and release the Holy Spirit, how can we teach God's young people? Young people don't have the layers of flesh that the enemy uses to cover up our God-given gifts. Young people can sense there is more. They are interested and open to dreams, visions, prophecy, revelation and other forms of communication God makes available to us.

In the 1970s, God's people were praying for revival. What if God delivered revival through a bunch of long-haired hippy freaks? I often wonder how many of those "freaks" opened the gift. Maybe they knew everything we never knew we needed? We may not mean to hurt anyone, but we cannot give away what we don't know we have.

I'm not sure why Jesus chose us to represent Him here on earth. I fall short every day, but I have the same yearning inside as young people. We are created in His image, and we are spiritual beings. People will find a spirit, either the Holy Spirit or one that comes to kill and destroy. Satan knows how to make his spirit look really cool on the outside, but his spirit is counterfeit and it leaves our young people empty, lost and hurting on the inside. Many times, they're empty enough to take their own lives.

We have the original and only God. The enemy does not even have omnipresence, the state of being everywhere at once. Satan will never be a match for God.

If we are God's hands and feet, we must walk and reach out to His children! How many more of His people are we going to let satan have? His children and our children need the Holy Spirit here on earth! If *all* people knew how to communicate with the Holy Spirit, there would no longer be a desire for the dark spirits of this world.

Other than food and shelter, the next thing God's people desire is to belong. Young people don't choose gangs, they just want a place to belong. Together we can open a place in the church, in our hearts, for God's people to belong. They may not look like us or smell like us or, better yet, act like us. They may have long hair, earrings, tattoos and all of the other distractions this world can bring. But if you look closely enough, you may see Jesus in them. Our Father gave us Jesus to create a place where we can belong. It's called Heaven on Earth — and that's what I call a party!

Whether we're young or old, sin is never the right choice, but it doesn't have to be an issue between us and God. Jesus dealt with our shortcomings — past, present and future — when He died for our mistakes. We can come boldly before the Lord at any time — even when we have fallen short, even when we are disgusted with ourselves, even when we have given satan power in our lives. Nothing we do can make God stop loving and caring for us! Hebrews 4:16 reads, *"Let us therefore come boldly unto the throne of grace, that we may obtain mercy and find grace to help in time of need."*

There is nothing you can experience that Jesus did not suffer on the cross. Please don't wait to get *everything* right before you walk with Jesus. If I had to wait to get everything right, my entire life would be gone and I would have missed out on the greatest friendship ever.

The Bible says we are one in Christ. To me that means everything we do—good or bad—we share. It doesn't matter how many times you have messed up or how bad your mistakes have been. What matters is that Christ died for our faults together. Sin is all the same to God. Together we can learn how to give our burdens to Jesus to look more like Him as we give His love to one another.

When we mess up, our flesh is influenced to instinctively turn away from God. We have to train our mind through God's Word to **stop** and turn back to Him in thankfulness. The value of our life was never based on all of the things we could do right. The value comes from what Jesus and His Father did for you and me.

If you're like me, you don't want to break God's heart or make Him worry about us. Let's keep as much sin as possible out of our lives for Jesus. And when we fall short, together we can pick each other up in love, and that alone will please our Father.

The party is just beginning, and we are all invited because every saint has a past and every sinner has a future!

It's time to open your Gift….

Chapter 3

Open the Gift

Good morning, Lord. Thank you for this day and all that is good. Take my heart and give me yours, and bring the people into my life who need to hear your *words, not mine.*

These are the first words I speak each morning. The last part of my prayer is most important: "not mine." I've learned many lessons over the years. One hurdle in my life is that I had to get over myself. I don't mean to let my life get in the way; it just happens. The ways of this world and even religion can lead us to believe we're not worthy to teach the truth about Jesus if we have sin in our lives. But in 2 Corinthians 5:21, I hear something different: *"God made him who had no sin to be sin for us, so that in him we might become the righteousness of God."*

As I've studied the Bible, it is clear that if sin—that is, our mistakes—keeps us away from God, and none of us are without sin, then no one could share the Good News. What if Mother Teresa had let sin keep her from caring for God's people? Sin was important to her because she used it to bring people to Christ. It may not have been her own sin, but it was "the way" to the promise for the people God loves.

We are the people God loves! The gift for me is understanding that the very sin in our lives will help us understand and teach His Truth. When you have fought the battles, you build up experience—and I admire God's people who bring experience.

So each morning I thank God and accept His heart, which leads me to the next part of my prayer. I ask God to send me an appointment. With all of my shortcomings and my experiences, I boldly ask Him to **send** someone into my life—someone who needs a word of encouragement from Him. The details are not important to me. I believe that if I ask, God will **send** someone and He will give me His words at that moment. I do not need any special skills, I just need to be willing—and as I live my life and as I walk along, God shows me.

Mark 13:11 says, *"Do not worry beforehand about what to say. Just say whatever is given you at the time, for it is not you speaking, but the Holy Spirit."*

When I first started working for my dad's printing company years ago, he asked me which project was more valuable: the business card or the multicolor brochure. I was so excited to get the answer right! "The color brochure," I said confidently, and told him all the reasons why.

I can still see his eyes as he smiled and said, "The brochure is beautiful, and it is worth more money. However, the business card is just as important to the person ordering it.

"Bobbie," he continued, "we may never know the people this card will touch."

I've never forgotten this lesson—one of the many seeds my dad planted to prepare me for God Appointments.

Please know this is not *my* book. It belongs to God. He is inviting you and me to share in His appointments. I am not a writer, a pastor, a teacher, a scholar, or someone you'd ever think courageous enough to step out of line. Today I am stepping in faith with God.

I'm going to share a simple Truth. In fact, it's so simple you may miss it. When things are simple, many times we overlook it or miss the meaning, so please read with an open heart, ready to receive. At times you may not want to continue, because you think you already know the message. That's the perfect reason to keep reading, because *we don't always know what we think we know.*

Satan has a way of making us think we have to be brilliant to understand God's promise. Matthew 13:19 says, *"When anyone hears the message about the kingdom and does not understand it, the evil one comes and snatches away what was sown in his heart."*

So don't be fooled! Satan focuses on what we think we know. But the *treasure* is found in what we do not know.

In the natural I know who I am in my mind and body, but for most of my life I didn't know who I am in the spirit and in the authority I've been given in Jesus Christ through the Holy Spirit. Discovering this *treasure* brought Heaven on Earth to my life and gives me **awareness** of the ways the enemy holds us captive.

The Bible tells us that we have the same spirit on earth as we will have in heaven. This is interesting to me. So the only thing holding us back from producing the fruit of the Spirit one hundred percent of the time is us—our mind and bodies. Galatians 5:22-23 says, *"But the fruit of the Spirit is love, joy, peace, patience, kindness, goodness, faithfulness, gentleness and self-control. Against such things there is no law."* Is that not the most powerful information you've ever heard? Against such things there is no law!

I just read in 2 Corinthians 5:17, *"Therefore, if anyone is in Christ, he is a **new creation**: The old has gone, the new has come!"* We know when we receive Christ, our body and mind does not change. The change is in our spirit, now filled with the Holy Spirit, which will remain with us in Heaven. He doesn't say we get a new body or mind while we are here on earth. This is the reason we have to renew our mind each day in the Word, the Bible, so we can be aware of our new spirit and understand what we have been given for Heaven on Earth. Satan does not want us to uncover the **power** of the spirit Jesus left for us here on earth.

The Bible says we won't have full understanding of our spirit until we are in Heaven. For years I accepted this and thought about how sweet it will be to have full understanding of my spirit in Heaven. The problem is that I didn't ask anyone about the Truth and "understanding" of the Holy Spirit I was missing **here on earth**. I was sure that other people had figured out the "here on earth" part of the spirit. I believed in Jesus, I knew I had the Holy Spirit in me, so why was I not experiencing the power or seeing the fruit in *my* life?

I believe most people who love Jesus are not experiencing that kind of life, either. It's just not enough to know of the Holy Spirit. Even satan knows that much.

Rather, now that I understand that the Holy Spirit is the voice of our relationship with Jesus and His Father, I see it's about communicating with God in *His* language. If we don't know how to communicate in *His* Spirit, how can we hear God's voice?

In my search for answers, God led me to many different teachers. My good friend Terri introduced me to the teachings of Andrew Wommack. Through Andrew, God made it clear that the Spirit He gave me is what gives me life. Andrew helped me understand how good and bad exist in all of our lives by illustrating that we are all made of three parts—body, soul/mind and spirit.

1 Thessalonians 5:23 says, *"May God himself, the God of peace, sanctify you through and through. May your whole spirit, soul and body be kept blameless at the coming of our Lord Jesus Christ."*

I knew who I was in my body by looking in the mirror, I could think and acknowledge who I was in my mind, but I didn't know how to release the Holy Spirit within me. I needed a spiritual mirror—something that would tell me how to communicate and listen for God's voice. (See James 1:22-25.)

The Bible is our spiritual mirror, and in faith we can trust what it says about us. Faith is simply the act of trusting what you cannot see. The Bible says we are righteous in Jesus, and that is the Truth. The Bible also says we are filthy rags in soul/mind and body, and that is also true—before we are made new in Christ. John 6:63 says, *"The Spirit gives life, the flesh counts for nothing. The words I have spoken to you are Spirit and they are life."*

So we have a choice, then: to focus on the Truth or on what was true *before* Jesus died for us. I hope you pick Truth, because what we focus on grows. If we focus on what we do wrong or what others are doing wrong, that is the direction we will grow. But when we focus on how much God loves us and what we can do right, this is how our lives will grow, and our desire to sin will lessen. We never will be entirely rid of sin until we leave this earth. Yet when we accept God's love and forgiveness, we can become holier by chance than if we try to do good deeds to earn holiness. An amazing example is how Jesus loved His disciples, even with all of their faults each was willing to go to the ends of the earth and even die because of the love Jesus gave them.

The message is pretty simple, and we need to keep it that way. The Father gave his son, Jesus, and Jesus gave His own life. People too easily forget what has been given to them. We have received the life Jesus gave—a life given purely out of **love**.

Quite simply, we love God through Jesus in thankfulness, and we love who He loves—all the people in this world!

If I focus on all the billions of people first, I get weary. But if I Love God first, His love will flow through me to love others. When we get off-center from the truth of His love, we open ourselves up to satan and a life of defeat.

Satan can influence our mind, and he can influence our body—but he cannot touch the Holy Spirit in us. It belongs to God and is supernatural. In Christ, our dead spirit is made alive by the Holy Spirit. Sounds simple when it's laid out that way, right? It is a simple truth—yet I had missed it for a long time.

Knowing what we've been given in the Holy Spirit and not releasing it is like having a trillion dollars in the bank but not knowing the account number to make a withdrawal. It belongs to us, but we can't use it.

I had a similar feeling when I thought about salvation, the forgiveness of sins and eternity in heaven. I knew I was saved, yet I felt I was missing something important here on earth. I felt I had a beautiful gift and yet I didn't open it to see what was inside. My prayer is that the words on these pages will help you open your gift (the forgiveness of your sins and eternity in heaven) and release what is inside (the Holy Spirit) to live out Heaven on Earth.

God loved us so much He trusted no one except His Son to bring this gift to us. His Son, Jesus, died painfully in the process, yet He did it willingly for you and me. I believe Jesus died because He knew how much His Father loved us and longed to have the relationship that satan took away in the garden. I also believe that being forgiven and going to heaven are more than we could ever deserve—but God gives us even more. The relationship is what Jesus wanted to give back to His Father. *Give back*...that's it! That's the reason I wanted to understand who I was in the spirit...to *give back!* I wanted to learn how to give back through the Holy Spirit what Jesus gave us in giving His life.

I needed to understand the depth of why He gave his life and, most important, what He left behind. I'd never known such a sacrifice here on earth, and that is how the enemy keeps us under his authority. Satan can use only what we know in our mind and body. He is not the author of anything except confusion, deceit and lying. He cannot understand the language of the Holy Spirit. He takes what Jesus left behind— the Holy Spirit—and keeps it all covered up in our body and soul/mind. He knows if we cannot hear God's voice, we will live limited by what we know in our minds and what satan also knows.

Untying the Bow

I received the gift of salvation at age 12. It was beautifully wrapped, and I looked at it every day with thankfulness. I thought the package was the gift. I didn't know something was inside.

In my forties, I went on my first mission trip, to Brazil. Soon after, I went to a place that changed my life forever: Africa. This is where I sponsored my first orphan and where God took my heart and gave me His.

On these mission trips, Doug Ehrgott, global team builder for Horizon International, begins each morning with team devotions. One of his favorite sayings is, "We cannot talk to people about God until we talk to God about His people." Through this experience I learned about awareness and how God works and loves through us, His people.

Each day in Africa, God let me experience the loss and loneliness these kids face. The sacrifice of God's love became so great in my life, I had to seek shelter to stand the pain. Each night I'd ask, *How can I ever make a difference, Lord?* I was just a girl from a small town in Michigan who had been given a gift. I was willing to give away the gift if it would help. But I couldn't see how the gift of forgiveness, salvation and heaven alone could help others or give them direction **here on earth**. The pain I felt came not just in Africa, but everywhere else God took me. I recognize now that through this pain He was preparing me for future God Appointments and to understand the language Jesus left behind.

Now, it made sense to me that I was saving the gift for heaven. I didn't know I needed what was *inside the gift* — that is, the Holy Spirit — if I wanted to experience Heaven on Earth. I was still blind to what was *inside* the package. Hebrews Chapter 11 tells us that faith pleases God, Faith releases God, and Faith moves God. Again, those words are great and powerful, but I didn't get what faith *looked like*. It was like a great big puzzle, and all the pieces were there before me. But I wasn't sure which piece went where. There's an old saying: "When the student is ready, the teacher will appear." I realized that I was available to learn, and God would use His appointments to teach me.

I knew I was saved **from sin**, and now I was going to learn what I was **saved for**. I would need to study faith in order to release what Jesus left for me here on earth, according to the

Scripture. Hebrews 11:1 reads, *"Be sure of what you hope for and certain of what you do not see."*

The true gift, the Holy Spirit, was inside the package — and my faith would give me eyes to see. Once I discovered why God gives us the opportunity to experience Heaven on Earth, I began to see His perfect plan and understand the importance of God's private language. I could **see** heaven and forgiveness as a gift to us **from God**, and I could **see** Heaven on Earth as a gift to God **from us**. It is our turn to *give back* what satan tried to take away. What amazes me most is that even our gift back to God saves His children (us) — another incredible fact!

In this world are places where people don't know God the Father or Jesus! The **only** reason missions can and do exist is because people still don't know God exists. Where we find true worship for God, we will find people who are not willing to leave one life behind.

Worship to God is not about what we get, such as forgiveness of sins and eternal life in heaven. I'm learning that worship to God is about what we can give back to Him in serving His heart for the harassed and forgotten of this world. Within God's mission, His people — the workers and laborers, His hands and feet — will find the true heart of Jesus!

I'm also starting to understand the difference between the eternal Joy of the Bible and temporary happiness/sadness of this world. Happiness and sadness will always come from external factors like friendships, weather and how we look and feel today. Eternal Joy comes from within and is released when we are working on God's harvest. In this process of *giving back* we experience the Joy of Heaven on earth.

Does it seem unbelievable that we have a Father who created an earthly system that never leaves us out? We should be inspired to give back simply because God gives us forgiveness and eternal life. But there is more! As we **give back** to God, He delivers blessings back to us in the process. God never stops giving when we have eyes to see.

Let me be clear: Motive matters! We do not give to get back. So many times I hear people say, "I'm praying, going to church and trying to do all the right things. Where is my blessing?" Can you see the motive in this question? I can see it because I'm guilty of it. When my motive is for the Glory of God, the action becomes supernatural, unexplainable by natural laws. *The eyes through which we give are the same eyes through which we can see the blessing.*

Another amazing revelation! What we focus on grows....

Here I was growing for all these years, and I was becoming tired of myself and even of the precious gift God gave me. Could it really be that He gave me the gift to open it and give it away here on earth?!

Jesus "gave away" His gift of life. To Him, He gave away more than His life. He also left behind, at Pentecost, the gift of the Holy Spirit. His life gave us forgiveness of sin and eternal life in heaven. The Holy Spirit gives us our relationship back with the Father here on earth...*Heaven on Earth.*

Remember, the Bible says our spirit will be the same on earth as it is in heaven. If that's true, the only thing holding us back here are our mind and our body. How convenient that is for satan, because those happen to be the two things he can influence.

With this understanding, the foundation of my life became clear: knowing who I am in the Holy Spirit and learning how to communicate in faith to release God's power. In turn, we do not give because we *want* — we give because we *have*. But we cannot give what we do not know we have.

Have you ever wondered why some people seem to have *more* of everything? I thought it was because they were better, more deserving, or because God loved them more. I'm aware now that I was thinking from my mind and the experiences of my body. I didn't understand how God created us and how He has no favorites. We are each His favorite and the measure of His Spirit is given as He determines. Together we are equal and lack nothing because we are one body. (See 1 Corinthians 12:11-12.) It is we who measure with our mind and cover up what God has given us in His Spirit. I call this "heavy flesh"!

When we learn to celebrate the success of others, we can find true success—God's heart—within ourselves. Success in the Kingdom is much different than the success of this world. When we don't care who gets the credit, the motive of His Spirit can shine through.

It's easy to be jealous when we see God working through others. That always happens when we measure, and someone always loses out. When we focus on what others have, we look away from what God has given us. This gives the enemy the perfect opportunity to take from us. We cannot see God in others until we can see God in ourselves. We cannot forgive others until we can forgive ourselves. We cannot stop judging others until we stop judging ourselves. We cannot stop measuring others until we stop measuring ourselves. Satan knows we cannot do this on our own; it takes the Holy Spirit within us to accomplish all of the above. Without the truth of God's unconditional love we will continue to see others based on our perception, on how we *think* God sees us.

Cutting the Tape

Jesus, God's only begotten son, was sent by God the Father to reflect Him. When Jesus came up from the water after He was baptized by John, He saw the Spirit of God reflecting on Him. (See Matthew 3:16.) Jesus was directed by His Father, and yet He had a choice—just like we do. I hope you are seeing how Jesus also was tempted by satan and how He had a choice to sin.

But He is the only one ever to walk the earth who died to His flesh—mind and body, one hundred percent. In His righteousness, He was the final sacrifice God used to end our suffering once and for all.

Jesus lived and walked with the disciples to teach and train, just like God the Father walked with Jesus in Heaven. Jesus came to hang out and experience life before He would tell; he knew the importance of taking time to build relationships. I believe Jesus raised the value of *mentoring*, or showing, in a culture of *marketing*, or telling. Thankfully He left the Holy Spirit to guide, encourage, walk and communicate with us.

Ultimately, God Appointments are nothing more than walking with God's people to **market**, or teach, the example Jesus left, through a relationship of *mentoring*. We're not to learn and keep our lessons to ourselves; rather, our lives are about giving away what we have been given. You will learn and experience Jesus as you walk with His people. Jesus truly gives us more than information; He gives us demonstration.

Some appointments will be proactive, through everyday kindness and knowing what the Bible says. Others will be reactive, directed by the Holy Spirit through revelation, or thoughts. This knowledge was critical for me to experience. I've had to learn how to hear the voice of God and understand that when the Holy Spirit leads me, *all* other plans for that day — or for my life — come second.

This is where choice, or free will, really comes into play. I can look back on each of my appointments, proactive or reactive, and there was a *decision point* for each one. Believe me, I have missed many appointments out of fear or because I wasn't listening for the voice of God. I continue to pray that my free will, would be so submitted to His will, that it looks like one.

The great news for God's kingdom is if I'm not available, He will find someone else who is. He will use people who are living their lives in faith, not in fear.

God Appointments are not about God needing us. They are about God loving us and wanting us to experience the true *privilege* of His love flowing through us to others. They are about building a church without walls in the heart of each person.

This is what we were made for and the only thing here on earth that will bring us authentic joy and fulfillment. When we allow God to love His people through us, we forget about ourselves and are transported back to the Garden, when Adam and Eve did not yet have knowledge of their mind and body. A time when they did not have free will and the Glory was in the will of their Father.

The enemy tells us through our flesh that we are happier when we serve ourselves. Many people do not have a choice because they are limited by what they know in their mind and body. Remember, satan knows what we know. He does not know what God knows and he does not understand the language God communicates with us through the Holy Spirit. The problem is **most people** do not understand how God communicates with us through the Holy Spirit.

Jesus died for our sins, for our rights to Heaven and to restore the spiritual relationship here on earth by leaving us the Holy Spirit at Pentecost. (See Acts 2:1-4.) With the Holy Spirit, God spoke His Word through prophets, apostles and disciples to write the Bible, just like God spoke through Jesus to teach and train the disciples. The Bible teaches us how to imitate Jesus in our everyday life. The Holy Spirit leads us to the divine connection God has planned here on earth.

Keep in mind, the enemy also knows the Bible, and without the Holy Spirit we remain limited under the authority of our body and mind. I say "limited" because the enemy can manipulate our understanding.

Satan is frightened of what we have been given through the Holy Spirit. He could not influence Jesus, and he is aware of the authority of the Holy Spirit Jesus left behind. The only reason satan has power here on earth is because we give it to him.

When God made us, we were spiritual beings. Our minds and bodies were directed and protected by God's Spirit. In the garden, satan tricked Eve into thinking she needed to have the same knowledge as God. And when Adam and Eve ate from the **tree of knowledge**, which God had forbidden, that sin took away their intimate spiritual relationship with God. They became aware of their bodies and thoughts because they no longer were covered and protected by God's Spirit. From the first bite, they became spiritually separated from God and immediately longed for His Spirit to protect them.

After the Spiritual relationship was broken, I believe God took Adam and Eve out of the garden because of love. He knew if they ate from the **tree of life**—also forbidden by God—in their current condition, they would be forever dead in their spirit and would have no chance to be reunited in Christ. Can you imagine your children being taken away forever and no hope to communicate with them?

God never lost hope in restoring His Spirit, His means of communicating with us, and offering us eternal life. He never stopped trying to protect us, even from ourselves. Even in our state of continual sin, God never leaves us. (Think about that for a moment. Isn't that amazing?) Even before Christ, He was faithful in His love for us. He spoke through prophets, gave us signs and even built a tabernacle where He could dwell and be available to reach His children. In spite of all God's faithfulness, the people in the Bible let their flesh get the best of them. And that is true of us today. Without knowing who we are in the Spirit, our mind and body get the best of us every time.

The Old Testament law prepared God's people through animal sacrifices to see they could never make it without a Savior. In the New Testament, Jesus died as the final sacrifice. In so doing, He gave us back our Spirit connection back. That's the *gift* I keep referring to. Jesus lived, loved and died to reveal the love He shared with His Father *and* to give that love to you and to me. The gift Jesus left is our direct line to Him and His Father. Again, the New Testament *revealed* what was *concealed* in the Old Testament.

Slipping Off the Wrap

Something wasn't making sense to me. I was understanding the Bible better, but I couldn't see Heaven on Earth. How could we be whole in Christ while most people, myself included, are living compromised and defeated lives? If we really got the garden back by gaining a spiritual relationship through the Holy Spirit, why weren't we acting like it?

Most of us talk a good talk, but our behavior never lies. The answer, I believe, is that most people do not know how to communicate with the Holy Spirit. More than ever, people are defeated, depressed, overwhelmed and addicted to anything that will help them forget who they are in their mind and body.

As I studied my Bible, I was conflicted. I was missing something. I read about salvation, forgiveness and heaven — and that all made sense. I kept hearing about Heaven on Earth, and the Bible says we have everything we need to fight the enemy. Yet I felt I was in a battle without any weapons.

Today I know the missing weapon was *inside* the gift. With the Holy Spirit, there is no battle — Christ has already won the war! 2 Corinthians 10:4 says, *"The weapons we fight with are not the weapons of the World. On the contrary, they have divine power to demolish strongholds."*

I wasn't missing anything after all; I just didn't know what I had. The real test of my faith was to believe the Bible's words about who we are in Christ and what's available to help us serve God and protect His people. The only way we can experience Heaven on Earth is to know how to release His Spirit.

Now, the Spirit is supernatural; we cannot feel it. Our flesh — that is, our mind and body — is natural and cannot understand the Spirit. (See John 3:5-8.) The Spirit will show itself through our mind and body when we are willing to be led by it. First we study His word through the Bible and communicate by praying in the Spirit, and then we wait for His voice through revelation and thoughts. This simple truth allows God's people to see Him in us!

God is concerned for each one of us, and that means we should be concerned for each one of His. This is what makes my life so exciting; I get to spend each day practicing with Jesus. Believe me when I say I'm not very good at this. But Jesus is a Divine Champion, and He continues to teach me and practice with me. He'll do the same for you.

Have you noticed that God's people are not always loveable? But if you have eyes to see their spirit, you will see true beauty beyond what this world teaches. This takes time and practice. Sometimes I think, *Dear Jesus, can anyone else take this appointment?* And most of the time He says, *No, no, no! This one is for you!* And He gently reminds me the treasure is sometimes hidden deep within.

Always remember: A setback is an opportunity for a comeback! Jesus waits for us to come back through the Holy Spirit!

In faith we must strive to see ourselves the way Jesus sees us — not how the enemy sees us. To the crack addict or alcoholic, satan says, "You are a failure. How can you even call yourself a man or woman in Christ? You are not worthy of forgiveness!" With thoughts like that to taunt us, of course we fail. Instead, we need to lift all the worldly restrictions that are placed on us by the enemy and *believe* that Jesus lives inside of us and sees us in His fullness through the Holy Spirit.

It does not ever get better; it's not about getting **more** or stronger in the Lord. We are as strong as we need to be.

Our church experiences may teach us to want more of Jesus — to thirst, to hunger, to be desperate for Him. But the only way we can be *desperate* for God is if He is not within us.

Satan wants us to think we have to hunger, thirst or be desperate in order to find God. But all we need to do is release what we've already been given in Jesus Christ and simply bear His image.

I believe we can be hungry for the understanding of His Word. The enemy can block the understanding of the word through our minds, but he cannot touch the Truth — the Holy Spirit, — within us.

Our Spirit does not have any desire to sin and make mistakes. It is one hundred percent righteous and redeemed. Our flesh is what has to be retrained. God's people need to stop saying, *I am sick. I'm tired. I'm hurt.* Our words should be, *I am healed in the Spirit; this is my right in Christ. Satan is the one who comes to kill and destroy through sin and sickness.*

We *are* healed and made well in thankfulness! Now we need to start acting like it by reflecting the truth about us and reveal our restored image. The enemy's greatest deception is keeping us unaware of what we have in Christ, what He left behind in the Holy Spirit.

Many people who believe in Jesus are cautious of the Holy Spirit. The enemy also uses the Gifts of the Spirit against us. The master of deception influences man to make the Gifts seem weird and intrusive. (See James 3: 13-17.) But the God I experience is kind, gentle and never intrusive. He never forces anything on me. When I used to read about the Gifts of the Spirit, speaking in tongues and healing, I would skim over those parts. I had enough challenges, and I thought I'd have to act strange to accept the gifts.

As time went on, I continued to study. God brought people into my life, like Andrew Wommack, Pastor Doug and Terri, my Bible study leader. They were planting seeds of Truth in my mind, and my heart was being prepared to become a woman of purpose.

Several years ago I was at a Joyce Meyer conference. Joyce, if you're not familiar with her, is one of the world's leading Bible teachers. At this conference, she taught about praying in the Spirit and the sacrifice God gave in His son Jesus so we could receive this gift. For the first time in my life, I understood what was *inside* the gift! I wanted *everything* that God gave me; I wanted His best. We were made to worship God in Spirit, and there's nothing weird or strange about that.

This was it! This is what I did not know! This was the language Jesus left to communicate with Him and His Father Jehovah.

Almost instantly I stopped thinking about what *I* wanted to tell God and what *I* thought I needed. I found peace in knowing what God wanted and what He needed to tell me. I found my home in a place I'd never been before.

When I speak about praying in the Spirit, to be honest I seldom say "praying in tongues." The enemy has put such a bad connotation on that phrase. In many cases like this, people have taken God's Word and added their own rules and regulations. Again, I am not an expert—but I cannot argue with the way my life changed when I began praying in the Spirit.

I come to you boldly because I have experienced supernatural God Appointments through this relationship. You'll read about some of them in the journals that follow.

Before you decide this is all too strange, try to hear me out. You and I each have a personal relationship with God, and we can pray to Him in the Spirit one-on-one. Of course, I also pray with my regular language. But if the enemy can understand and influence my mind and body, he can influence what I think I need or want from God. If we are willing to pray from our body and mind, could it hurt to also pray from our Spirit? John 4:24 says, *"God is spirit, and his worshipers must worship in spirit and in truth."*

What allows me to take personal prayer to a whole new level is to know the enemy cannot understand my communication with God in His Spirit. I don't even understand my prayers, thank goodness. If I did, I would probably mess it up with my limited thinking. Romans 8:26-27 confirms to me, *"In the same way, the Spirit helps us in our weakness. We do not know what we ought to pray for, but the Spirit Himself intercedes for us with groans that words cannot express. And (God) who searches our hearts knows the mind of the Spirit, because the Spirit intercedes for (us) in accordance with God's will."*

The gift I receive by praying in the Spirit is the path God provides through revelation, or thoughts. (See 1 Corinthians 14:13.) God reveals to me in ways I was not able to receive before I opened my heart to this level of praying.

But let me be clear: My prayers in His Spirit are *personal* to God, and I **do not** need to pray in the Spirit with anyone or for anyone. God's revelation, His direction is all I desire when I pray in the Spirit. After all, why would we need to pray for or with anyone else when the direction is for ourselves? To think otherwise is to believe the food we eat can nourish another body, or that the air we breathe can bring life to another person.

Praying in the Spirit is as personal as intimacy with our spouse! We have to receive this personal, life-giving prayer so we can then go out and *give* life by serving God and delivering whatever He reveals to us for His people.

Removing the Lid

Remember in the Bible when Jesus asked Simon, "Who am I?" Simon answered, "You are the son of God."

Jesus changed his name to Peter, which means "rock," on which He would build His church. I believe God built His church on the *revelation* — the thoughts from God Peter had, not the man Peter was in his flesh. (See Mathew 16:15-18.) Revelation from God is the most powerful weapon we'll find on this earth.

Now, we can have Godly thoughts without praying in the Spirit. We also can get food from a feeding tube. But nothing can take the place of God's best! I believe God intended for us to have a *private prayer language* with Him — a closed-circuit channel through which He reveals knowledge that we cannot understand in our flesh and that cannot be understood by the enemy. This knowledge can be interpreted only in our spirit. And released, **made known** through our mind/soul and body.

He offered the best in His Son, and He offers the best in our relationship with Him through the Holy Spirit. We are the sons and daughters of the Most High God, and we need to claim our Father and protect His Name. In doing this, we offer Him our very best.

Knowing how much God loves us is important. But the real joy of Heaven on Earth is allowing God to love His people through us. This desire was given to us from the beginning of time, and nothing here on earth can substitute. We have all tried to find fulfillment in the areas of our mind and body, and we always find ourselves wanting. That's because our flesh is motivated by the desire to fill our emptiness, which can never be filled. Love motivates us by the joy of sharing our fullness, which is making God known. Satan comes to pervert the life giving Love found in 1 Corinthians 13 to a self love that destroys. I believe we get to Heaven through salvation alone, but why would we want to miss the relationship here on earth that Jesus died for?

I am thankful to understand that God's people are made of three parts: body, soul/mind and spirit. This allows me to see that we all have sin in our lives. I have learned when we focus on who we are in the Spirit, our desire for sin lessens. If we do something wrong, we can still love the Lord. We simply have a body and mind that can be influenced by this world. Our sin has nothing to do with His Spirit. The Holy Spirit in us is marked with a seal by God. Ephesians 1:13 says, *"And you also were included in Christ when you heard the word of truth, the gospel of your salvation. Having believed, you were marked in him with a seal, the promised Holy Spirit."*

This doesn't mean we are free to go out and sin. (See Romans 1:1-2.) Rather, we should know that what we focus on grows. People know when they've done something wrong, and with prayer, love and forgiveness they can get back to their spirit to make God known.

I confess my flesh continues to distract me, and most of the time I can't blame the enemy. I still sin, and there is a price to pay for that here on earth. Even though we are forgiven in Christ, sin hurts the people around us and takes away their hope. It also influences us to turn away from God. But God can and will use our mistakes to build His Kingdom.

I encourage you to come boldly to God in His Spirit. We have access to God even though we have sin in our life. God sees us in the Spirit. We see ourselves in the flesh, and we tend to act out the bad image the enemy has placed on us. But if we could see ourselves in the Spirit like God does, we would act out His plan for our lives.

We all have the same opportunities to shine for God or to sin. It is time we reach out to others like Jesus reaches out to us — without judgment. Jesus was not jealous of His Father's love for us. He died for His Love. We only have to die to our flesh, which is to deny our body and mind/soul. The Bible tells us to renew our mind/soul each day in Christ. (See Romans 12:2.)

I have come to understand why we need to read the Bible and give God the first of our fruits. It is important to be in the Bible each morning so we can renew our mind in the Spirit and tame our flesh. Throughout the day, our flesh will try to resurrect itself. Our flesh knows it has a short time here on earth, that it was born to die. So it lives for today, for the senses, utterly unconcerned about eternity. It is not going with us to Heaven and has no respect for life after death.

My life changed when I realized the "self" was never meant for us. It is a false image, given when sin entered the world. Our original created image was love. Jesus came to remove the false image, and His life on earth demonstrated who we were created to be. When we study the life of Jesus, we are actually studying our God-intended nature. Anything else is a lie from satan.

Years ago I was invited to hear a gentleman from Africa speak at a local church; his name was Jackson. He said that every once in a while he has to give his flesh a talking to. "Look, flesh—you were born to die, and you are not in control!" he'd say. "You'd better get back in line. I am living for eternity, and I am not taking you with me!" I smile even now when I think of Jackson. Try repeating his words sometime—but maybe not in public.

God doesn't want us to use our minds and bodies as an excuse to fail. He gave us the Holy Spirit so we could live a life not bothered by our body and mind. He wants us to have constant worship with Him through our Spirit. Our body is not good or bad; it is neutral, following the mind's influence. The problem comes when satan gets involved, and he comes to kill and destroy through both body and soul/mind.

Hold firm, because God knows our struggles better than we do. Through Jesus, He took on every sin for us. Nothing we go through wasn't already experienced by Him on the cross. Jesus took on our appearance after sin, so we could once again look like who we were created to be.

Our flesh does not want to die; it wants to live in peace as it once did in the garden. Our minds and bodies were victims of sin, and the only way we can protect them on earth is to learn how to live in the Spirit. Remember what 2 Corinthians 5:17 tells us: *"Therefore, if anyone is in Christ, he is a new creation; the old has gone, the new has come!"*

All things are new in Christ. Note that all things have become new — not *are becoming* new. The Spirit is not a work in progress. It's all there from the time we make Christ our Lord and Savior. Your mind and physical body don't change when you receive Christ, because you look the same in your flesh. Your spirit is what changes. John 6:63 says, *"The Spirit gives life; the flesh counts for nothing. The words I have spoken to you are spirit and they are life."*

From the moment we are saved in Christ, we spend the rest of our lives renewing and retraining our minds by reading the Bible and believing in faith what we've been given in the Holy Spirit. Learning God's language helps influence our flesh to accept the spiritual relationship we had in the garden.

Peeking Inside

You've never seen your own face, right? You've only seen a reflection of your face in a mirror or in a photograph, and you trust that the reflection is real. This is the way we have to see the Bible. Our mind has to trust it like our flesh trusts a mirror. James 1:23-25 says, *"Anyone who listens to the word but does not do what it says is like a man who looks at his face in a mirror and, after looking at himself, goes away and immediately forgets what he looks like. But the man who looks intently into the perfect law that gives freedom, and continues to do this, not forgetting what he has heard, but doing it — he will be blessed in what he does."*

Whoever looks into the Word of God and believes what it says about us is like a man looking into a mirror. We look at our faces in the mirror enough times to trust what we look like even though we've never seen our own face. We must look to God's Word enough to trust what we cannot see. The only way we can trust the spirit is to read the Bible and believe in faith what it says about us. For me the Bible is a mirror for who I was created to be, not a microscope to see others.

I admit, sometimes I feel the power of Jesus in me and sometimes I don't. Yet even when I don't feel the Holy Spirit, I know it is there. In our spirit, we have all the glory of God already in us. (See John 17:22.) It is like our "sixth sense" — the faith in Christ in us, so deep it surpasses our natural understanding of it. Philemon 1:6 says, *"I pray that you may be active in sharing your faith, so that you will have a full understanding of every good thing we have in Christ."*

We cannot be depressed and defeated if we fully understand the glory of God in us. In the physical, life is full of problems. But we can overcome times of trouble, times when we don't feel the power and glory of God in us by understanding our spirit. Again, once we are saved through Jesus, we spend the rest of our lives renewing our mind to what we've been given in the Holy Spirit. The sooner we can believe and trust, the sooner we can experience the power of God.

Again our bodies are an exact representation of what our mind/soul is thinking. If we have everything the Bible says that we have in Christ and our body still sins, a third thing must connect them — our mind/soul, our thoughts. Our mind can build us with Christ or break us with satan. It always comes back to the same starting point — what is driving our thoughts?

If the Bible, the Word of God, is where we turn to glimpse our spiritual mirror, our thoughts and our spirit will be one with God and the body will follow. When we lack the influence of the Bible, our body can persuade our minds to behave against the spirit. No matter how bad life may get, it's never too late for us to come back to our spirit. We always will be God's *treasure*, even when we cannot see.

Understanding how we were made allows us to release the Holy Spirit that dwells in us and experience God's best by praying in the Spirit. I'm still learning, and there's so much I don't know. But I cannot argue with my changed life. I do not want you to live God Appointments through me. You are unique and special to God. There are people waiting to experience God's love through *you*. In the daily devotional I read,

God Calling, one particular passage stands out as a beautiful message from God. The words express how deeply He wants us to spend time with Him and deepen our relationship with Him through the Spirit. The passage reads:

"My children, I am here beside you. Draw near in spirit to Me. Shut out the distractions of the world. I am your Life, the very breath of your soul. Learn what it is to shut yourself in the secret place of your being, which is my secret place too.

True it is, I wait in many a heart, but so few retire into that inner place of being to commune with Me. Wherever the Spirit is, I am. Man has rarely understood this. I am actually at the center of every man's being, but, distracted with the things of the sense-life, he finds Me not.

Do you realize that I am telling you truths, revealing them, not repeating oft-told facts? Meditate on all I say. Ponder it. Not to draw your own conclusions, but to absorb Mine.

All down the ages, men have been too eager to say what they thought about My truth, and so doing, they have grievously erred. Hear Me. Talk to Me. Reflect Me. Do not say what you think about Me. My words need none of man's explanation. I can explain to each heart.

Make Me real, and leave Me to do My own work. To lead a soul to Me is one thing, to seek to stay with it to interpret mars the first great act. So would it be with human intercourse. How much more then, when it is a question of the soul, and Me, its Maker, the only real Spirit that understands it."

From *God Calling*, published by Barbour Publishing, Inc. Used by permission.

Testament of Devotion, by Thomas R. Kelly, is another beautiful book that reinforces this message.

Everyone has an opinion about how and when the Holy Spirit comes to you. Some people claim you get it when you accept the Lord as your Savior. Others say you have to pray again for the Baptism of the Holy Spirit, and only then do you receive it. Whether you pray to get or release it, just pray in faith that you have everything you need in the Holy Spirit.

I know I have it. I know He is alive and living inside of me, and I know things I couldn't possibly know without His Spirit.

Sharing the Gift

Earlier I mentioned that I knew a simple truth, so simple you might miss it. Please, if you get nothing more from what I've shared, I pray you don't miss this.

I trust like my next breath that we can go to Heaven and have our sins forgiven when we accept Jesus as our savior. Salvation is for eternity.

Letting the Holy Spirit work through us is a choice—our choice while we are here on earth. The Spirit is gentle and respectful, just like Jesus. The Holy Spirit is not going to drop down, kick you around and make you do crazy things. But you have to give utterance, you have to take a step, and you are responsible to meet God.

After I understood what it meant to pray in the Spirit, several weeks passed before I actually did it. It was easier for me to tell myself I didn't have what it took. Don't be fooled by this thought. You have it if you have Jesus! The enemy tried to convince me that praying in the Spirit had no more value than the childlike chatter we make up as children. Maybe it is our childlike faith that allows us to practice and prepare with God.

Move ahead in faith! Go to a quiet place and give God your beautiful utterance. Do not let the enemy make you feel uncomfortable. You may sound strange, but I believe God hears His language as beautiful music. The first time I prayed in the Spirit, I know He was proud of me for what I could do. Now I've grown to love my time with God in His Spirit.

Our God is a God of order. When we pray in the Spirit, we are edified, instructed, so we can hear His revelation, His voice. Some people think and act differently when praying in the Spirit; I attribute that to personality styles or expectations from flesh.

As for me, His Spirit has always brought me peace. I've never leapt from a church pew or yelled in the middle of a crowded room. I know what I've experienced, and I am pleased. I will remain open and continue to be a learner and a server.

God makes room for all of us. Together we can make room for all God's people to worship. In all we do, let us remember that our God is a **God of order**. Let's respect His house and all of His children.

I admire Apostle Paul's behavior for God. In the Bible he spoke in the Spirit more than any other follower. Paul understood that praying in tongues was for his personal relationship with God. It did not edify or enlighten the church body. In the church or with God's people, Paul said it would be better to speak one word of understanding to God's people than many words in the Spirit. 1 Corinthians 14:18-19 helped me see Paul's heart for God's people: *"I thank God that I speak in tongues more than all of you. But in the church I would rather speak five intelligible words to instruct others than ten thousand words in a tongue."*

Understanding is a gift. Together we need to be aware and protect God's people so He may deliver the truth of the Holy Spirit. It makes sense why Paul wrote so many books of the Bible. The only reason I want more revelation from God here on earth is to love God's people. We need to give because we *have*, not because we *want*. Know that when we give for God through faith, we have everything we need and *more than we deserve*. I hope we encourage each other and can love because we are loved; we can forgive because we are forgiven.

Jesus said we could do great things in Him. (See John 14:12.) Through revelation, God empowered me to write this book. I was asking God if there was a way for me to work full-time in missions. On the way to the gym I was praying in the Spirit. During my workout I was talking with a trainer about my God Appointments and how I was learning about the power of the Holy Spirit. Out of left field he said, "Bobbie you need to write this sh— down." I looked up at the ceiling, and the voice in my head said, "I want you to write a book." I said out loud, "Okay, Lord!"

Keep in mind that this book includes only a few of my God Appointments. Each one is a treasure from God. But the real treasure for me will be to hear about your God Appointments!

My dad used to say, "Bobbie, if we each do a little, no one has to do a lot." Together we can each do a little; together we can help God love His people. Together with the Holy Spirit directing us, we can bring Heaven to Earth.

The world is full of people waiting for us to show up and **be** the God Appointment. Each "package" will look different. Some won't even have a package. Through the Spirit, you will know when and how to show each appointment the image of Christ. The blessing for you is showing them how to open the gift so they can join us in our God Appointments.

You will not be alone as you begin to receive appointments. I will continue to pray and ask God to trust us with His people. I will pray for you and the lives you touch. In advance I say, "Thank you, my dear friends!"

I will wait to hear about your God Appointments on www.godappointments.com. Remember, you have everything you need with your experience plus the Holy Spirit.

We are one in Christ...and "Total Trust."

Chapter 4

Total Trust

From the moment we are conceived we make an imprint on someone's life. With each breath and each decision, the effects are known. We don't always get to see them, but the effects are there. Even after we die, our decisions can change lives here on earth.

At times I wish I could have started my life with the end in mind. Today I know the end is never "the end." I love that it's never too late to start over, and today is always the perfect day to make a new start.

The perfect day for me was early October 2009, when God directed me to write *God Appointments*. Now, I know there are far better writers than I will ever be. So for me this book represents trust—the trust I have in God's ability to work through His people. It did not start the day He told me to write; it started the day I was conceived.

Through relationships we learn to trust. This process takes time and much communication. We can choose when and with whom we want to communicate. I have grown to trust that when we communicate in a way that is pleasing to God, He releases His Spirit within us.

*I don't want my life to be measured by the number of breaths I take, **but by the moments that give God's breath away.***

This eight-year journey started in July 2003, two years before my father passed away. "Daddy, when do I slow down?" I asked him.

He replied, "Bobbie, do not slow down until every child is fed." *This moment gave God's breath away.* His words seemed familiar in my spirit, and yet my mind was **not ready** to trust.

Four years later, in July 2007, I was preparing to go to Africa for the first time with a short-term mission team. I didn't know the agenda for this trip. Our mission pastor, Doug Ehrgott, invited the founder of Horizon International to share his organization's vision and details of our upcoming journey. Bob Pearson had formed Horizon to care for children orphaned by AIDS.

At our meeting, Bob shared his own story, which included his Divine Appointment with God to give hope to AIDS orphans—one child at a time—using sponsorships to **feed**, educate, build families and grow God's kingdom. *This encounter gave God's breath away.* Bob's words seemed familiar in my spirit, and yet my mind was **not ready** to trust.

A few months later, I went back to Brazil on another short-term mission trip. Our team attended a church service in one of the communities we serve. We arrived late—tired, sweaty and underdressed for the occasion. We sat at the back of the church, where I could barely see the pastor. But to my surprise, he could see me. He moved toward me and, in a language I couldn't understand, he spoke directly to me. As people glanced my way, the pastor's voice grew louder. I looked around for support or guidance or understanding, not sure what was happening.

Our interpreter, Paulo, spoke Portuguese and began to interpret the pastor's words, giving meaning to the revelation hidden deep within my spirit. As the pastor looked in my eyes, he prophesied a ministry that would grow around the world. *This moment gave God's breath away.* His words seemed familiar in my spirit, and yet my mind was **not ready** to trust.

One year later in 2008, I'd returned to South Africa with Horizon International when God called me to talk with an African couple cleaning the lodge. The couple shared how they left their children for months to make money to feed them. As I told them how fortunate the children were to have parents who cared, the man interrupted me. His gentle nature transitioned to a posture of strength and boldness as he looked intensely into my eyes. He said that God had sent me to Africa and people needed to know what I knew. People were beaten down and needed hope, he said. He grabbed my hands and encouraged me to speak the message. He said something about "radio around the world."

One of my teammates said the encounter reminded him of the evening in Brazil, when the pastor prophesied a ministry around the world. *This moment gave God's breath away.* The African man's words seemed familiar in my spirit, and yet my mind was **not ready** to trust.

In April 2009 I was on my way to Zimbabwe to speak at a women's conference. Deciding to go to Zimbabwe was one of the most difficult decisions I'd ever made. Looking back, the spiritual warfare that took place before this trip was as great as the treasure I found there. As my team arrived at the conference area, I saw women lining a dirt road, crying and cheering. Many of the ladies had walked for miles, hours, days — with children on their backs. *They have been repeatedly harassed and then forgotten by this world, but not by God!* I thought.

I am forever grateful to the women of Zimbabwe.

My next thought jolted my heart. *Dear God, is this a part of the ministry you were talking about?* I was halfway around the world speaking to the ripe, the available, the people I now know to be God's harvest. God was giving me the privilege of serving His best while planting another seed of trust in my mind. I hear and I forget, I see and I remember, I do and I understand. *This moment gave God's breath away.* His words seemed familiar in my spirit, and my mind was **being prepared** to trust.

In October 2009 after praying in the spirit, I was talking with God. I mentioned that if there was a way I could do missions full time, I was available. Within one hour God answered. He put a very direct thought in my mind: "Write a book." *This moment gave God's breath away.* His words seemed familiar in my spirit, and this time my mind was **ready to trust**!

"Lord, You know what I have and if that is what you want, it is yours," I said.

I knew the only thing I had to give Him were my God Appointments. I pulled the only two journals that I had recorded from under my bed. *Are you sure, Lord? I can barely write my appointments down on paper, much less form them into a readable book. Lord Jesus, it would be easier to move a mountain!*

Several weeks went by and I began to write about some of my appointments from memory. The book began to take some sort of shape. I told a few friends that God had told me to write a book. One friend joked, "People always say God told them to write a book." But then he said, "I wonder how many people God has *really* told to write a book?"

His words gave me doubt, but I knew that if I were to write a book, it would be God's doing. I kept my journals close and pledged that I wouldn't worry about the particulars. When God gives us an assignment, He gives us everything we need to complete it.

The good and the bad news is that our faith brings everything into His plan. But this is where we can get tripped up. It was easy for me to have faith and believe, because I've been taught as much for most of my life. "Believing" is a safe place because it doesn't require action or responsibility. It gave me a false sense of contentment with my life and allowed me to focus on my limitations or what I cannot do. More important, I wasn't getting to experience what God could do through me.

Yes, I have limitations, fear and moments of doubt, and I know who I am without Jesus. The problem comes when I let those things be an excuse not to let the Holy Spirit work through me. I read in the Bible that I can do all things through Christ! The difference is now I **trust** what I believe God can do through me. This new way of thinking allows me to get over what I am *not* and trust that I can practice with God each day and become what *He is.*

When I have moments of doubt, I read 1 John 4:4, *"You, dear children, are from God and have overcome them, because the one who is in you is greater than the one who is in the world."*

As I prayed in the spirit, I realized *God Appointments* was going to need a beginning. It amazes me how God gave me one picture at a time — just like His Appointments with Joseph. He gave him one dream at a time, enough to take another step to protect Mary and baby Jesus.

With direction from God, I knew to begin by explaining what brings me God Appointments. Again, God gave me something I could do. Just like when Jesus asked the woman at the well to give Him a drink of water.

Do you see yourself in the life of Jesus? You and I are in each occurrence throughout the Bible! We continue to create new chapters as we live our lives. The people are different, but the message is the same, and His mercy never fails.

The first chapter of this book, "Open the Gift," was written in several sittings. I never know necessarily when it's going to be time to write; I don't plan it, I just know when it happens. The more I write, the more thoughts God gives me. When I go back and read the words, they sound like they belong to someone else. As I wrote this book I knew I was in the middle of a miracle, and in faith I knew there was no end — only eternity. I experienced Heaven on Earth.

Days would pass, and I wouldn't write a word. By late October I was getting ready to go to Africa with my sister Lisa. Her relationship with Jesus had just begun, and we were experiencing the normal battles that come when you're connecting with God. We were together for several days on the trip, and I was amazed by how God communicated through her. Words that flew from her mouth took me by surprise. She was becoming a new creation before me. The old was gone, and I was interested in her renewed Spirit. She also was praying in the Spirit and sharing what God put on her heart through revelation. Lisa told me I needed to take this book seriously, that people needed to know what I knew. This was beautiful, but I was still trying to figure out what I knew.

The gift of sisterly love... I was listening to you, Lisa, all along.

Soon after we returned home, she became more persistent, calling almost every day to ask if I was working on the book. Some days she'd call back to apologize because she knew I was busy with work, family and life. The next day she'd start a conversation with "I am sorry" and then say, "Bobbie, you need to get this book done."

I had witnessed her faith and seen how she communicates with God. I needed to take her seriously, because I knew where the message was coming from.

One day she asked, "Sis, do you have a website? God put it on my heart that you should have a website where people can log their own God Appointments."

I told her if God gave her that thought, He would give us the person to help at the right time. Another day she called and just when I thought she was going to mention the website, she blurted, "God told me this morning the book has to be published in every language!"

"Of course," I said drily. "I will let the publisher know."

My life is funny because God makes me laugh. I can see Him in His people; they are beautiful to me.

Several days later, He gave me a thought of God Appointment Break (GAB) bracelet. This would give people an invitation when they saw someone wearing a GAB bracelet to ask about their God Appointment. I could envision young people, students, moms, dads, pastors, people all around the world wearing GAB bracelets. *Go GAB!* I thought. (I won't blame this one on God; I think this silly thought might be from me.)

A few months later in March 2010, I was preparing for another trip to Africa, this time with a group of young students. Silvana, whom you'll read about later, was going with us. She came to stay at my home a few weeks before the trip so she could meet the whole mission team. I told her I was writing a book, and she asked to read it. Moments later, she yelled to me, "Bobbie, this is amazing! You need to keep writing. People need to know this stuff."

Again, I thought, *What is it that I know?*

I told her about my sister's website idea. "I know how to do that," she said. By the end of the evening she had set me up with a website. I was surprised and yet not surprised. God gives us everything we never knew we needed—every time. Why should we be surprised when He does what He promises?

Once again, my life got busy. Our daughter Robbie was expecting her second child, and our daughter Billie was going to South Africa with me. I had no extra time, yet I was receiving more God Appointments than ever.

By the time we returned from our trip in April 2010, the book was taking shape. My friend Theresa—with a journalism degree—had helped me get all of my raw thoughts on paper in a readable way. I'd been sending her my writings, straight from the thoughts God put on my heart to my hands to the keyboard. I didn't worry about my grammar and all the stuff that distracts from my thoughts. I wrote with no inhibition.

Theresa would take my work and, with her gentle way, encourage me to give more and more. I continue to thank her for her belief in me, but she reminds me that God has given her an assignment, too.

God has given me each detail of His plan for this book. He even gave me the name for our ministry. His plan was stored in my spirit until my mind was ready to **trust**. Early one morning I was lying in bed, staring at the ceiling when the thought flashed in my mind, "Life After Sin." Immediately I thought, *What do those initials stand for? L.A.S....* And *the next moment gave God's breath away...*Testimonies! Life After Sin Testimonies. His words seemed familiar in my spirit, and I TRUST like my next breath that God has inspired L.A.S.T Ministries.

"Who is going to publish your book?" is one of the top questions I hear. I typically say that God told me to write the book and He'll take care of the details. It's wonderful to watch people's faces when you share faith with them. Try it! I've trusted God in faith to have everything I need, including the words. I've trusted myself to have faith to **release** God's plan.

One day at work I stumbled upon the name "Zondervan" in a list of sales contacts and wondered if it was a publishing company. Now I know many people recognize Zondervan as a giant in Christian publishing, but I'm not the kind of person who usually notices things like this. I didn't give it another thought until Billie gave me a study guide on the Book of Esther. I turned the book over and saw "Zondervan Publishing."

The next day over breakfast, I grabbed my Bible and did a double-take. I saw upside down "Zondervan" broken up in three parts–ZON DER VAN. I laughed out loud because just a few days earlier I was unaware, and now it seemed to be jumping out at me everywhere I turned. I went to a bookstore to inquire about a particular children's bible called *The Adventure Bible* that I wanted to buy for the orphans I would visit in Africa. I asked the store manager if we could get a discount. He said, "I have a good friend at Zondervan. I'll see what I can do."

By this time, I finally had to ask the question, *Lord, is this the company you want to publish your book?*

At this *moment in time* the publisher may or may not be Zondervan. I've learned that God's plan is open and never ending. The one thing I'm sure of is Jesus lives inside of me through the Holy Spirit, and He spoke to me through revelation to write this book. I know who the Author is, because I have a personal relationship with Him.

We do not need to know the future. We just need to know that God will send us. I hope you will come — and *give God's breath away*, I **trust** and believe.

It's not about a lack of belief or believing more…. It is about *trusting* what you believe.

Enjoy the journals.

Chapter 5

Hope Lives and I Am Alive

I'm sitting here with my eyes shut, my fingers on the keyboard, thinking how and why I can possibly share my past when I've spent so many years trying to cover it up.

But when I feel God calling me to do something I *don't* want to do, that's when I know I *must* do it. Through experience I've learned that each of these difficult moments is the perfect opportunity to show God my faith, even when I am scared out of my mind. And like my dad always said, "When we don't want to do something is when we need to do it." Many times I rolled my eyes when he spoke those words. Now I can smile because I know something amazing waits on the other side every time.

This journal was not written for *God Appointments*. I originally wrote it as I was preparing for a mission trip to Zimbabwe, where I was scheduled to speak at a women's conference. The event was not just for any women, but for women who have been harassed and forgotten by this world. We'd been asked to pray about our testimonies and the details and messages we should share. As I focused on this task, I knew God was calling me to give away something I'd been trying to hide for a very long time.

In this process God revealed to me how the very same story can bring life as well as death. Whenever separation occurs in a relationship, there is always more than one opinion, more than one set of eyes, more than one experience, and more than one appointment.

I may appear to be the victim of the story I'm about to share, and for years that's how I would have described myself. But this morning on my way to catch a plane to New Jersey, God gave me new revelation.

On the drive to the airport, I decided not to turn on my music but instead use my quiet time to pray in the Spirit. I told the Lord I didn't need anything and asked if there was anything I could do for Him. I wasn't prepared for His reply.

"The book is not finished," is what I heard. Then, "Bobbie, you are gentle like a lamb *now*, but you were tough as nails *then*."

I knew right away what He wanted.

He then brought back lyrics He wrote through me a few years ago:

"I give you all my burdens; they seem too hard to hold.
Not for you, my friend, my Jesus — to you they are like gold.
Without the weight of this old world, you
make me who I am.
Let them see the Christ in me, your mercy to the end."

With God's gentle nudging, I thought back twenty years to a very different time in my life when I did not know how to give my burdens to the Lord. At the time I recorded this experience for the Zimbabwe conference, I could only see through my eyes. I thought this story was about abuse and one victim. I'd already forgiven the person who hurt me, and I thought that was enough.

Even though I have prayed in the spirit for many years, I now have a new understanding of how closed our minds can be to receiving God's word. The Bible says, "Oh Lord you have searched me and you know me." (See Psalm 139.)

Confirmation came through a friend who explained some-times it's not just about forgiving someone; it's about asking them for forgiveness. I had never asked the other person in this story to forgive me. It has been twenty-one years, and this was the first time I was able to receive God's word in this area. A verse in the Bible says, Ask and you shall receive. (See Matthew 21:22.) Today I received not because I asked. Today I received because I could understand God's language....

—

My husband's hands were around my neck. *This is it,* I thought. *I am going to die.* I pleaded with him, and the more I screamed and fought the harder he choked me. With my last breath I said, "Lord, *please.* I will be good."

In that foggy moment, I wondered who would raise my children and whether they would know how much I love them. I thought about my parents and how this would shatter their hearts. I even thought about my husband and how he wouldn't want to live once he realized what he'd done. Then, every thought vanished as my world went black.

Later, I woke up and realized I was alive. "Thank you, Jesus," I cried out, again and again and again.

Up to that point, I felt like I'd made so many bad choices and taken many wrong turns. I had no sense of how much God loved me, nor did I know how or why I was forgiven for my sins.

Yes, I had grown up in church and I believed in God. I was baptized at age twelve and taught Sunday school until I was fifteen. I loved my parents and wanted them to be proud of me. Yet I hadn't come to believe God could forgive me for the things I'd done even as I tried to make the right choices.

My life changed forever the year I turned sixteen. That's when I discovered I was pregnant—by my first and, to that point, only boyfriend. I met him in sixth grade, and by junior year in high school we were engaged. Shortly after that, I became pregnant.

Not wanting to face the truth, I denied it to myself for six months. I didn't want a child. And most of all, I did not want to tell my parents. I felt I would rather die than face them with my shameful news. So I thought instead about the different ways I could kill myself so no one would ever know. The enemy planted thoughts that my sin would hurt my parents more than the loss of my life.

I am thankful God knew who I was in Him even when I didn't. I thank God that He loves each and every life, even the ones who don't come in a perfect package.

My daughter, Billie Lou, was born just weeks before my seventeenth birthday. From the day she was born, God has used her life to reach and save others.

But Billie's dad saw her only the first few months of her life. He turned away from his young family and toward drugs. He didn't have much use for us.

The next several years were tough. My perfect little life was gone, and I didn't know when or if I would get it back.

But there were unexpected blessings. My parents stepped in and welcomed Billie like she was their own. Not once did my sisters — Lisa and Jamie — or my brother Shawn show jealousy or resentment toward the newest member of our family. Their reaction to this unplanned life would become one of the greatest lessons of my life. Even in sin, my family made me feel valuable. Even in sin, we are a treasure to God.

*My sister Jamie, my little brother Shawn, my mother,
Bonnie, and my sister Lisa demonstrated what
the love of Christ looks like here on earth.*

To tell this story fully, I should share the words my dad spoke the morning after he learned I was pregnant. Remember, this is the same father I would've died to protect from pain and shame. He opened the door to my bedroom and found me there crying. He smiled and gently said, "Please never forget that a life is always good. When you love someone like the love in the Bible, it doesn't matter what they do because you will always love them." God shows up in His people! He is everywhere if you have eyes to see.

When Billie was two years old, I met a man who would become my husband. He came from a good family, and I felt fortunate that he would want me and my child.

Our first year together was great. He was a hard worker, he loved Billie Lou, and he was crazy about me. I fell easily into my new role as a wife and mother.

My new husband traveled during the week, working as a welder on big moveable bridges. Every Friday, I'd eagerly await the sound of his truck pulling into the driveway. We were a good team and enjoyed our life together.

Then another milestone birthday came—my twenty-first. To celebrate, my husband threw me a surprise party. That evening was one of the few times I noticed him drinking hard liquor instead of beer. After our guests left, I cleaned up the house while he paced the floor, breathing hard.

He started to question me and demanded that I stopped cleaning up the house. When I didn't, he grabbed my straight, long hair, twisting it around his hand and pulling me to the ground. Later that night in bed, I wept and wondered, "Do I deserve this, Lord?"

The next morning he was full of sorrow. For days he begged me to forgive him. I did, and he promised never to drink liquor again. I trusted that he would keep that promise.

When I became pregnant with Robbie Sue, my second child, things were good again. My husband stayed away from alcohol and I had hope for the future of our family. We had our share of hard times and good. But the funny thing about good times is that they can hurt worse—because they hint at what could be. When my husband wasn't drinking, he was wonderful. His goodness compelled me to forgive him, time after time.

And some part of me still believed I was paying for the mistakes I'd made earlier in my life. Jesus died for sinners, I knew, but somehow I didn't feel included. All of the people who attended church seemed perfect, but I had so many secrets and thought I could never measure up. I told myself that he would change and one day I would be good enough. For seven years I believed this, living for the day I would finally measure up. Then came the night I took what I believed was my last breath.

Instead I woke up—*alive*—and said to God, "I will be good."

The truth is, I didn't know how to be good for God. I had a kind heart—I always have—and treat people with love. But I had no understanding about the Spirit inside of me.

Soon after, I took my daughters and once again I walked away from rejection and pain. I wanted a new life and a chance to find peace. Even in this decision, I didn't actively reach out to God. On top of all my other mistakes, I was adding "divorce" to a growing list. *God must be so disappointed in me,* I thought.

During this time, as I reflected on my life, I remembered the peace I felt as a child. Before sin and shame entered my life, I never wanted to hurt anyone and never believed someone would want to hurt me. The words my dad said, when I was sixteen and pregnant, came back to me: "A life is always good."

Did God think my life was good?

I wanted—*I needed*—a new start away from years of pain and loss. My next step in life happened with help from Diane, a high school friend who lived in Indianapolis. The city seemed like a nice place to raise my girls. There I felt safer, but peace was yet to come—probably because I continued to search for wholeness in the wrong places. I met a nice man who, after a few months of dating, asked me to marry him. I did not get married, because I recognized I was with him for the wrong reasons.

I thought about my most desperate moments, when I promised God I would be good. I started taking my daughters to church. Week after week as I listened to Pastor Tommy, his words spoke life into me. He told me I was vulnerable, and that the enemy wanted to kill and destroy me so I couldn't work for the Lord. He told me I must take what satan meant for destruction and use it to build God's people and serve His Kingdom. He taught me about forgiveness, how we should be thankful for what we know and who we are in Christ—and never forget the words Jesus spoke from the cross: "Father forgive them, for they know not what they do."

God had already forgiven me. He made me for a purpose. At last, I was receiving the Word! I found the Lord again. He had never left me; it was I who had left Him. Pastor Tommy has since passed away. I wish I would have told him how much his life meant to me. He always made me feel like the message was straight from God just for me. For the first time in my life, I felt Him in my heart and I fell in love with my life. I fell in love with His life—that is, the Holy Spirit—in me.

Even then, I couldn't see that taking my children and moving away would hurt my ex-husband deeply and seriously affect the rest of his life. For twenty-one years, **God waited** for me to accept this God Appointment.

When at last I called my ex-husband in faith to ask for forgiveness, I wasn't entirely sure what *I* needed to be forgiven for. Then I heard his voice say, "Bobbie, I cried every time the kids had to leave"—and for the first time I could feel both his pain and the love God felt for him.

When we take God's heart, we can know in faith that each heartbeat brings an opportunity for a new relationship. Receiving my ex-husband's forgiveness that day was a gift I didn't know I needed. The Holy Spirit led me to take my eyes off the wrong and transform into what Jesus made right through forgiveness.

Our family has grown since that moment. My ex-husband married a beautiful woman and has helped raise a wonderful stepdaughter; he is a good dad and loves his family. I married a kind, gentle, supportive man. For more than fourteen years, my husband, Brian, has been a committed stepfather to Billie and Robbie and a wonderful "Pa" to our grandchildren. My daughters are amazing women with families of their own. We are blessed so far with six grandchildren and counting.

My life is not perfect, but it is peaceful because I have Jesus. The world can influence our minds and it can torture our bodies, but it cannot take our Spirit! God gave me a chance to take another last breath. I am thankful to live, and I am not afraid to die. Whether I die naturally or by force, I will use each remaining breath to talk about how much God loves us and how He saves us to multiply His children for eternity.

My family is truly everything I never knew I needed.
Seated, from left: Michael, Lenox, Billie Lou, Robbie Sue, baby
Corbin, Dayton. Standing, from left: Andreas, Keontaye,
Devon, Bobbie Suzette, Brian and William.

Chapter 6

A Father's Love–A Lifetime God Appointment

It's early in the morning and I'm having so many thoughts about love and what it really means to experience love. I remember hearing the expression "God is love" as I was growing up. Now I'm thinking about how we can be aware of many things, but actually experiencing them is a whole different ballgame.

I sat on the bench most of my life. I cheered for others and longed to be part of something great. Perhaps I didn't have enough confidence to get in the game, or maybe I was waiting for someone to invite me in.

In the same way, I'm learning to see things through the eyes of God. He has been in my heart for many years, but I never before asked for His eyes. I am learning that with His eyes and ears, I am part of something great...by being in "God's game."

I leave again for Africa in a couple of weeks. In preparation, I've been studying the book of Esther. Esther, if you don't know, was a Jewish orphan who was raised by her uncle, Mordecai. No one would ever have singled Esther out to save a nation. So why did God choose her? Was she smarter or prettier than all other girls of her time? Why did *she* stand out? Why did He ask her to get in the game? I've come to believe the answer is simple: Esther was on the bench; she was available!

I am grateful for my time on the bench. It's where I've learned the most valuable lessons. It's where God allowed me to become a learner and a server. At times I felt I was ready to play. Then after a few hurts and heartbreaks, I slumped back to the bench. But I never left the team; I just needed a rest, a renewed purpose. I needed to get into God's Word and believe what it says about me. I needed to have faith that God gave me all the talent He needed me to have. The bench is where God let me heal, rest and start over.

What you choose to do on the bench allows God to use your life. So many people look at their own lives as a waste. But remember that your life is not a waste to God, no matter how bad it's been to this point. You are perfect to show God's love whenever and however you make yourself available—on the bench or in the game.

When I was growing up, I might have been voted most likely *not* to succeed, by earthly standards anyway. But guess what? I decided to play on God's team. On God's team it doesn't matter if I'm on the bench or in the game. I win—*we win*—just by showing up, because we are one on God's team.

As I look back, I see that my father was crucial in developing my heart for God. He protected me by not letting me leave the game. I was shy, chubby and unsure of myself. My dad knew I wasn't ready to play, so he let me watch from the sidelines. It must have been painful for my parents to watch me get pushed around time and again as I stepped out on the field of life. But they knew I had lessons to learn on my own. Experience is the greatest teacher and even though we cannot always choose the teacher, we can choose what we receive.

It is so easy to love when everything is good in life. It's easy to be kind and positive when nothing challenges us. As I observe myself and others, I'm aware that the greatest opportunity comes when life is less than perfect, even when it seems hopeless. We need faith most when we cannot fix troubles on our own. (See Luke 6:32-35.)

One of the greatest lessons I've learned began with a phone call from my sister-in-law. She said my father had suffered a brain hemorrhage and they did not think he was going to make it. The only thing I remember is screaming, **"Don't let him die before I get there!"**

I am not sure there are words to describe the love I felt — *feel* — for my dad. He was my hero as well as my father. A stranger to no one, he showed a love for people that goes beyond what this world teaches. Even in his death at the age of seventy-two, he put others first. The most amazing thing is that he taught me more in the fifteen months of his death than he taught me during my life with him. I am here today because of his love. More times than I care to admit, the only reason I didn't check out of life was because I didn't want to hurt him. Love is the most powerful weapon we can use to discipline the people around us.

When I arrived at the hospital, I was told my dad wouldn't live through the night. His brain wasn't functioning and he couldn't feel or understand anything around him. The words made me furious. I insisted that my dad never gives up and would be alright.

Facts didn't matter; if I didn't get the answers I wanted, I'd ask someone else. We ended up taking my dad to several hospitals, including the Mayo Clinic. With each evaluation, the medical specialists announced the same prognosis. Each time, I'd tell myself, *They don't know what I know*, and move on. I couldn't bear to hear another person say, "Your father does not know you anymore."

What was wrong with these people? Why did it matter whether he knew me or not? People all over the world don't know God, yet God knows them intimately and loves them anyway. He not only knows each person's name, but every hair on their head, too.

The only fact that made sense was that *I* knew who my dad was — and if he didn't know me, that was even more reason to stand by his side.

When I was young and I'd tell my father someone didn't like me, he'd say, "Bobbie Suzette, that's because they don't know you." He then made sure I understood I had a responsibility to help others know me. It usually meant I needed to grow and change.

If my dad didn't know me, I was going to have to introduce myself to him again...not because I wanted something from him, but because I had something to give him. The same love that Jesus gave me even when I didn't know Him.

Finally, when there were no more doctors to call and no one else would listen, my mom suggested that we take my dad to a nursing home. I agreed it would be a good place for him to rest while he healed.

My mother was a pillar of strength through this process. Though my dad's legal documents made it clear he didn't want to be kept on life support, she knew he wouldn't want to leave if I wasn't ready to let him go. Against the lawyers' advice, she let the nursing home keep my dad alive.

During those long months, I was dedicated to finding a way to bring my dad back. The hemorrhage had been so harsh that the doctors declared him brain dead. I would hear their words and the Holy Spirit would tell me something different. Each day I would whisper in dad's ear, "You are going to be okay. I know you won't give up."

I spent long hours telling my dad about things I was researching and how his brain could heal. I knew he could hear me. After all, my dad was the one who taught me that if you don't give up, you will make it. Years later I found a verse that told me the same thing. Galatians 6:9 says, *"Let us not become weary in doing good. For at the proper time we will reap a harvest if **we do not give up**."* I love that verse for many reasons, but mostly because our heavenly Father wrote it and my earthly father lived it.

When I was growing up, my dad had several special signs he used to communicate his love for us. He had this beautiful smile and big blue eyes. His wink spoke a thousand loving words, and his thumbs-up was like a burst of energy. I never imagined how important these signs would become as he lay alive—but barely so—in the nursing home. In the mission field, there's a saying that ninety percent of the work is presence and ten percent is performance. In my dad's case, one hundred percent of his work was presence, because he had zero percent performance.

When my dad met my mom, she was a ballroom dance teacher. So we'd play music in his tiny room and dance. Our times together at the nursing home were a celebration, the room packed with family members and friends. Once a month my mom asked what I thought about keeping dad on feeding tubes. Each time I'd reply, "He is going to come back."

And even though she believed he'd never "come back," she let me cling to my hope. It reminds me of a prayer God gave me years ago: "Help me be strong when others are weak and, more important, help me be weak when others need to be strong." My mom became weak so I could be strong.

One afternoon while we were singing and dancing, I asked dad if he could hear us—and he winked! All of us in the room—my mom, myself, several other relatives and friends—yelled and screamed and cheered as if he'd risen like Lazarus from the dead.

Several days later, he gave us a thumbs up. Another time he snapped his finger. He also reached out to our newest granddaughter Lenox Lou.

I'm still amazed that with all of the feeding tubes, the smells, the drool, the gagging, the blank eyes and dad's distorted face, all we could see were those small things **he was able to do**. Is this how God sees us? With all of our shortcomings, He somehow chooses to see what we can do. He knows we are not perfect and yet He loves and celebrates us anyway.

Watching my father pass on over fifteen months turned out to be the most beautiful experience of my life. He taught me so much about the Lord during this time, and the way God never leaves us but carries us until we can walk with Him. I believe my dad stayed alive because we weren't ready to walk. Even in his dying, he was a way for God to love us through him.

On my dad's seventy-second birthday, November 5, we had a big party. The nursing home was quiet, and the other family members who'd come by to visit had gone home. I stayed behind to spend a little time alone with my dad before I went back to Indianapolis.

This day was different than the hundreds of others before it. I could see my dad for the first time. He was weak and tired; he didn't want to stay. For fifteen months I had my eyes on myself. I didn't want to face my life without my father, so I asked him not to leave. And he didn't. Doctors would tell me it was a miracle he was still alive. When love is big enough, the facts don't count. God's miracle to me was love — my father's love!

Now it was my turn to **love** my father, and I knew what I had to do.

I crawled in bed with my dad and put my arm around him tightly, tears streaming down my face. I whispered in his ear. "Daddy, if you are tired I understand." Speaking these words, and facing the truth of this moment, hurt so badly that I had to remind myself to breathe.

I stopped short of saying it was okay to leave; I didn't have the courage. I didn't want my dad to hear me crying, so I sat at the foot of the bed and held his feet.

"God, I will take care of him for the rest of my life if you let me keep him," I prayed. "But if for some reason you need to take him, I think I can make it now."

I thanked God for giving me this special time — and my father died before I could visit again.

My dad loved me enough to stay until I was ready, and his family and friends loved him enough to see only what he could do.

Of course, no one has ever loved me like Jesus! Even in my selfishness, He shows me kindness, and He waited patiently while I developed eyes to see. Now, my purpose is to say "thank you!" with the rest of my life through God

Appointments — simply letting God love His people through me and you.

My father, LaVerne taught me to give because I have.

Chapter 7

Going Without Knowing

Brazil was more than a mission trip for me. Not only was it my *first* trip, but it provided me a living picture of what obedience can bring to our lives.

I've always known that we are not meant to keep God's love for us to ourselves. We are all disciples, and we have the opportunity to ask God to bring us into the lives of those who need to see His love. I have tried to be obedient whenever I felt God trusting me to serve one of His people. For a long time I have been aware of appointments from God in many situations.

But during my trip to Brazil, away from the comfort and security of my everyday life, God revealed to me a bigger plan of what it means to go and serve.

My family had attended the same church for more than eighteen years, but we didn't know many people. I have always been cautious of the church taking me off the streets, away from the people I most desired to serve. I am not saying this was right, but it is a true part of my story. Looking back, I understand that God gives us seasons of service and I believe God was teaching me to build a church without walls in my own heart.

But during that time, God showed me how to love His people. He taught me that each life is special, with a unique

God-designed plan. He taught me to see people where they could be and not judge them for where they are.

As I continue to grow in my relationship with the Lord today, my love for His people only grows. This is the love I would like to give as I share my journey.

Several years ago, while attending Sunday morning church service, I heard an announcement about a special speaker. It didn't mean much to me, because I wasn't in the habit of going to those types of extra programs and services. That week, though, I left the bulletin on my kitchen counter. When I went to toss it away, I saw a note about the speaker. Something made me stop.

I asked Brian if he'd like to go. When he declined, I called my daughter Robbie Sue. She laughed and said, "Sure, I'll go. But why are we going?"

I said, "I don't know, but I am going!"

I couldn't tell you where the speaker came from, but it had something to do with a village that had flooded. During the program, I saw pictures of the floodwaters covering a **bridge**. That evening when a collection was taken, I took out my checkbook and tried to write the normal amount I'd give in these situations.

God had other plans, and another—much larger—figure gently dropped into my head. I tried again to write the normal, conservative amount, and at the same time I asked the Lord why He wanted me to give more. The feeling grew stronger, moving from my head to my heart, so I obeyed. I wasn't worried about how I'd come up with the funds—and God provided, as He always does. After that incident, my family and I went back to our Sunday-morning church routine and life went on.

Three years later, I was talking to my friend, Liz, who informed me that God put it on her heart that I should go to Brazil. My first thought was that missions people are always trying to get others to go on these trips.

Even so, I called the church immediately. Keep in mind, this was only the second extra activity I'd stepped in. *Why are you calling the church?* I asked myself. *You're not actually going on a mission trip!*

I learned in that phone call that the church was organizing a trip to Brazil and another to Poland. The Poland trip sounded interesting, yet I was compelled to learn more about Brazil. I felt safe in asking because all of my time was booked and I could easily say no.

I got the dates for the Brazil trip. A quick glance at my calendar told me those eleven days were the *only* open days in my schedule for several months.

The next week I reviewed the trip schedule. I told myself there was no harm in attending the first organizational meeting. Some people there looked familiar, but I didn't know any of them personally. If God wanted me to go, I would be there.

By now I'm familiar with how God works with me. He is gentle but persuasive. Most times He gives me signs I can understand. The only sign I needed this time was eleven people, eleven days. Countless times, I've gotten confirmations from God, seeing these very numbers at inexplicable moments. When I see them, I know God is giving me the blessing, comfort, nudge or peace I need at that moment. I've never asked for these numbers, nor do I depend on them to make decisions. We can only depend on the Holy Spirit through revelation in our own minds. So with or without the numbers, I knew God was calling me to Brazil. My husband also could see the signs that God was calling me.

So I went to Brazil.

I thanked God every day for His guidance and direction as I prepared and left. On the way, I received my next confirmation. We were running through the airport to catch our flight, and a gentleman on our team—a diabetic—had to take his blood count. I stopped to see if he needed any help. He assured me he had things under control and urged me to catch up with the others. I didn't feel right leaving and waited for him to finish. When he did, he said, "111." I asked if he got that reading often; he said he didn't remember having it before. Later on the plane, he confirmed that he'd checked his log and found no other "111" reading. Somehow I knew that before he told me. "I am here Lord," I said. "Thank you!"

In retrospect, I can see that God organized each detail of that trip. I felt secure in His plan and prayed I wouldn't somehow get in the way.

As we stepped off the plane in Brazil, I briefly wondered, *What happens if I don't get my luggage?* And, out of twenty-some bags belonging to our group, my personal luggage was the only one that didn't arrive. My other luggage—filled with supplies for Brazilian children—was safe and sound. My personal bag finally showed up the day before we left.

Surviving in Brazil for more than a week without my luggage was a whole new experience. I grew up with everything a girl could wish for, including great parents, many comforts and more than enough love. God used this situation to teach me about His provision.

The enemy tried to plant seeds of shame and guilt. He tried to make me think God was disappointed in me for focusing too much on preparing for my physical needs and neglecting my spiritual preparations. The enemy's influence worked on me for two days, but he couldn't negate the devotions pastor, Doug, revealed each day. By the third day I was back...with or without a change of clothes. The enemy's tricks would no longer work on me. There was a blessing in all of this, and I was beginning to see it. I had my backpack, camera, journal, sunglasses, vitamins, one tube of eye cream and, most important, my Bible. What else could I need? I was ready for the journey.

The next days passed like clockwork: breakfast, devotions and off to the local schools. Each day, we'd visit a group and use our singing, dancing, skits and testimonies to introduce the children to our friend Jesus. Life was good. I stopped longing for clean clothes and enjoyed every minute of this God Adventure. I wasn't yet hit by any lightning bolts from God, but I experienced plenty of beautiful children, schools, churches, pastors, pastors' wives and new friends. I felt a freedom I'd never felt before, even though I didn't understand God's reason for sending me.

I have to giggle when I think of how patient God is with me. Many small details slip past me, and I miss some of the information He needs me to have. I'm still not sure what I missed along the way, but three years after hearing the "special speaker" at church, He revealed His plan. God had put it on my heart to hear the speaker that night, to give more than I would normally would and eventually to go to Brazil.

One day in particular was great. I got to ride in the back of a big truck, close to the scenery with the wind on my face. As we drove through the area, I saw "1111" on many of the fences, but I didn't ask what that stood for; I already knew. Next, we drove over a **bridge** that seemed so familiar. I felt like I'd been there before but decided it must look like a bridge I'd seen at home.

The next few days were wonderfully rewarding. I even got to go shopping for fresh clothes and new undergarments, which enabled me to receive another unexpected blessing. Several of the women had told me I should pack bland clothes for the trip—like there's a universal somber dress code for all missionaries. I made the sacrifice and tried to conform to this standard, packing my bag with the most boring clothes I had. The Lord has never made me feel I had to become someone else to serve Him. Instead, I feel He needs each of us to be unique so we might reach and serve all of His people.

When it came time to shop, the only store was around the corner from the pastor's home. I went out with Vania, our interpreter. The only pants that fit were cropped jeans with pink ribbons hanging off the pockets. To top it off, I found a pair of platform sandals. I was back! Maybe I didn't fit the "missionary dress code," but I felt like the real me again.

Another great gift was experiencing this with Vania, an amazing woman who serves God with her whole heart. I don't know who had more fun, her or me. (I won't share our comments about the undergarments!) It was refreshing to discover that Vania was real and that even missionaries cut it up and have fun (thank you, Jesus!). I thanked God for keeping my luggage stuffed with bland clothes. I also let Him know I appreciated His sense of humor. What the enemy uses for destruction, the Lord can use for instruction.

Each day of the trip, we witnessed new miracles and blessings, including helping the pastor move into a new home provided by the church. We watched him and his family cry with thankfulness and joy and were greeted by children at the new church and school built with help from previous teams.

One unexpected evening, God opened my eyes and revealed the details I'd missed along the way. While Pastor Moises was preaching, he mentioned he'd visited the U.S. several years earlier to speak at our church. He explained that our congregation's generosity had helped rebuild the flooded village. My heart beat faster as I finally recognized Pastor Moises as the special speaker at the only event I'd ever attended at church! Now I knew why the **bridge** looked so familiar; I had seen it in his pictures. How could I be sitting here in this church three years later, half a world away and hearing this message? I felt as if my heart was going to burst. *This moment gave God's breath away.*

After church we went to Pastor Moises' house. I told him I had attended that service three years ago, and he smiled. There was no way I could explain to him how great God's love is for me and what was happening before my eyes. Who could understand the greatness — the complete significance — of this journey? I didn't understand any more than what was before me, but that was enough. I had the team, many signs and, most important, the understanding that I had been led by the Holy Spirit.

As the rest of my days there passed, I was amazingly peaceful. My luggage finally arrived and it was nearly time to go home. Our last meal in Brazil was at Pastor Alexandre's home. As I stood looking off the balcony of his home, I noticed an address across the street — 111.

"I am here, Lord. Just show me," I said.

My next thought was that I should give each woman there a hand massage before we said goodbye. It seemed to be a friendly, comforting gesture. I was careful not to miss anyone and felt pleased to give God's love away.

Walking out to the van at the end of the evening, I saw a woman who had been present at a church we visited in the mountains. *Where did she come from? How did she get here?* At the mountain church, she'd been holding a small child and staring at me through the service. As we were leaving the church, our eyes met and we seemed to communicate a shared bond. I thought of her later, and the special connection we had made. I'd wanted to see her again, and yet her church was so far away. So I thanked God for the appointment and asked Him to take care of the woman and her baby.

That last night, I met the same woman face to face in the dining room. I could hear the van's horn blowing, calling for us to get on the bus. *How did she get here? Why am I with her again?*

The world stopped and the noises went away. My friend smiled and handed her child to someone. I looked her in the eyes and took my hand lotion from my back pocket. I began to massage her hands, and she started to cry. I had to shut my eyes, because I too was weeping. My heart was breaking, and the Holy Spirit rushed through me like a river. I hugged her tight while we both cried…until I had to go to the van. I had no answers, just experiences — and I was leaving Brazil.

On the van, I overhead a conversation that we were going to stop and pray over land that was the intended site of a new church. I'll admit, I just wanted to keep driving. I was exhausted, hot and ready to go home. I hoped this would be the last stop.

We got out of the van and walked toward the location. Down a small hill was the site they'd picked for the church. My thoughts focused on the fact that it was hot and I wanted to leave. The prayer complete, our group remained to talk. Feeling quiet, I wandered down the hill. Though the air was so hot, I felt a sudden strong cool breeze. Looking around, I didn't see anyone's hair or clothes blowing, yet I felt an unbelievable, jarring breeze. I didn't want to understand any more about why I was in Brazil or what I was doing; I just wanted to be home.

I arrived home with no answers, just a peaceful feeling of obedience. Then, a few months later, God revealed the reason I went to Brazil: It was all about the future church — the one I hadn't wanted to stop and pray for. The Lord once again put on my heart to give more, this time to help build a church in Brazil. The provision came from money my dad left me when he passed away. My dad left me provision, and God turned it into prosperity!

Finally I learned that sometimes you just have to go to know. I am pleased with God's plan and the way He loves all of His people. Everything else about the trip was for me. He taught me how to release more, trust more, pray more and to love more. God gave me everything I never knew I needed.

Chapter 8

Faith Is Thicker than Blood

The other day I was talking with my friend, Diane, about God Appointments. She mentioned that everyone thought I was crazy when I went off to Brazil while my sister, Jamie, was "on her death bed." I was surprised—and a little hurt—to hear these words.

"Bobbie," she said, "you should tell that God Appointment."

Why would I want to tell anyone I left town while my sister was near death? Could I have been so selfish, focused on my own needs, that I didn't even notice my sister's? I spent the day dwelling on these thoughts and praying in the Spirit. After much reflection, I still didn't remember feeling worried or scared to leave Jamie.

That evening at home, I prayed in the Spirit again. I was all alone and eager to spend quiet time with God. Within minutes I had the thought, *Faith is thicker than blood.* (God always knows when something is on my heart.) I felt bad because I didn't know the true feelings of my family and close friends. My wonderful, nonjudgmental family and I have always agreed that sometimes we would disagree. We value our love for each so much more than any dislike or disagreement that arises. Maybe that's why no one shared their true feelings with me about my leaving for Brazil at a complicated time for my family.

This appointment started several years ago…with a dreaded late-night phone call from Jamie's husband, Tim. Something had gone wrong after surgery and Jamie's body was in septic shock.

"The doctors said the family should get here," Tim said.

Within minutes, I was on my way to St. Joe, Michigan—a three-hour drive away.

My brother-in-law was a Marine, has flown fighter jets and has traveled across the world on special missions. It takes a whole lot to rattle him. Even on the phone, I could hear the heartbreak in his voice.

I'd just began studying the connection between body, soul/mind and spirit. I had enough confidence in this new discipline that I'd pray over my sister and for her complete healing. After all, I knew who I was in the Spirit, right? I prayed most of the drive and felt like a rock when I finally arrived at the hospital. Tim said I could see Jamie as long as I promised not to lose control.

I walked in with my Bible like the great healer. The minute I saw her, I fell to the floor, gasping and crying. I grabbed my heart and begged, "No, Lord, not her."

Jamie is like a flower that is always in bloom. When she walks in the room, you cannot help but smile. She loves her husband and children like no one I've ever known.

The moment I looked at the hospital bed and saw someone who didn't even slightly resemble my beautiful sister, I lost all hope and faith. She was swollen beyond recognition. Her skin was clay-colored, and she had tubes in her throat and nose. Tim and my mom ushered me from the room and said I couldn't see Jamie again. Tim already felt helpless and couldn't take any more pain. He was searching for a way to protect her and keep her safe.

My mom, her sister Lucille, my cousin Penny and I went to a nearby hotel. Lucille was in one bed with Penny, and Mom and I were in the other. I rolled over in bed, thinking, *What am I doing wrong, Lord? I have no control over my emotions.*

I was in my flesh and didn't know how to get back to my spirit. I fell asleep praying for strength. In the morning I went into the bathroom and looked deep into my own eyes through the reflection in the mirror. My eyes welling with tears, this scripture overpowered my mind: "Be sure of what you hope for and certain of what you do not see." (See Hebrews 11:1.)

That was it. I was certain God wanted my sister here on earth, and I knew my faith would release His Spirit. I found renewed strength in what the Bible says and knew this time my confidence was in His Power.

Throughout the night other family members arrived. We were having breakfast together the next morning when my brother Shawn's phone rang. It was Tim. He told us to get to the hospital as soon as possible. Everyone began crying again, yet I wasn't moved. I assured them that everything would be fine. In my family, news travels fast. I'm sure they'd all heard about my wild-woman breakdown the night before in Jamie's room. With my calm demeanor, they must have been seriously worried about my mental health at this point.

At the hospital chapel, we stood in a big circle to receive the news. Tim told us the night didn't go as well as hoped. The doctors said Jamie's prognosis was not good. Feeling quite brave, I asked Tim if I could lay hands on Jamie to pray. His memory of my last episode had not left him, and I knew better than to push.

I moved on to Plan B. *No worries,* I thought, *God can work from a distance.* I must've looked like a cartoon character to all of them when I said I was going to pray. But sure enough, the Holy Spirit took over.

I thanked God in advance for healing my sister. I thanked Him for her life and all of His plans for her. I thanked Him for giving her kidneys the ability to cleanse her body and restore her to health.

When I looked up after the "amen," their expressions told me they were sure I'd lost it. One by one, each person returned to the hospital lounge. No one wanted to talk much, and that was fine. I knew deep down that Jamie was healed and had peace in this knowledge.

Tim said he was going to check on Jamie. I listened as my family members wept around me, my own strength growing. In fact, I felt out of place because I wasn't sad.

Not ten minutes later, Tim showed up looking like he'd been to the Mountain. His face was full of life as he said, "I'm not sure how this happened, but her kidneys are working now and she's breathing on her own." *This moment gave God's breath away.*

"Thank you, Jesus!" I said.

Tim told us about how one of the nurses hadn't tied down one of Jamie's arms after drawing blood. They figured that Jamie reached up and pulled her life-sustaining tubes out. When the nurses checked on her, she was breathing on her own and her kidneys kicked in at the same time—at the time we were praying together. The medical staff didn't understand how she had the strength, under sedation, to remove the tube. Through faith, I know she had help from our friend Jesus.

Tim sat down next to me. We both glanced at his watch, which read 11:11 a.m. I looked up at him and said, "I just want to hear that you know it was God."

"I don't know how it could be anything else," he replied. "I was with her before I met you in the chapel, and it wasn't good."

Then he said, "Sis, I didn't want to tell you because of all the hubbub, but last night as I watched her monitors, the reading was '111' throughout the night."

I know it took a lot for Tim to share this with me. But most of all, I knew he believed this miracle had come from God.

Jamie and Tim have three wonderful children. Their oldest, Zachary, was in the chapel during the prayer. Their two daughters, Dakota and Payton, arrived just after we received the good news. Zachary must have called Dakota, because she arrived with her arms in the air, proclaiming, "Aunt Bobbie, you brought Jesus!"

I'll remember her words as long as I live. Please know that we all have the choice to release Jesus in any situation!

Several days later, I left for my second trip to Brazil where I received the prophesy of a ministry around the world. Jamie remained in critical condition and had a long journey ahead of her. Her body slowly healed over the next several years.

Dear sissy, Jamie, this is one time I would have given you the front seat. You have taught me strength beyond yourself.

But when I boarded the plane for Brazil, I was certain of what I couldn't see and certain that God wanted me to go on that trip. Faith moves God; faith pleases God. Matthew 17:20-21 says, "*He replied, because you have so little faith. I tell you the truth, if you have faith as small as a mustard seed, you can say to this mountain, Move from here to there, and it will move.*

Nothing will be impossible for you." Faith healed my sister. In faith Jesus saved my sister, and in faith I went to Brazil!

Sometimes you have to go to know!

Chapter 9

Africa and a New Heart

In July 2007, I'd been back from Brazil for nine months. I was on my way to South Africa with Horizon International and was excited to spend time with the children there. Now, it may be hard to believe I was excited about visiting children who were made orphans by rampant AIDS. Our flesh can't comprehend what happens to create an environment where so many children are without parents. Anyone who witnesses the situation realizes the heartbreak of hunger and devastation of loss for the children left alone to care for themselves and for their siblings. For me, the excitement soon faded, and heartbreak replaced it.

One day I quietly wept. I found it hard to talk or even breathe at times. I spoke a sentence over and over: "I am giving you my burdens, Lord."

Again and again I would give away the pain in my heavy heart. I could actually feel my heart, separate from my body. I must believe that someone reading this has had a similar experience. I wonder if Jesus' heart felt this way when he was separated from His Father. When you love someone so much and you are connected spiritually, separation can feel like death. The greatness of the pain is in direct proportion to the greatness in which we have loved. Yet through this pain I have learned to thank God for my broken heart.

Each morning in Africa started the same way. Our morning devotions were a symbol of dressing for battle. Each day was a process of recovery—heartbreak by day and thankfulness by night. I wanted so much to be God's hands and feet, yet I didn't know He'd lead me to a place like this.

I never knew a place like this existed. No matter how much you read, watch TV or listen to news, you cannot know how your heart can become separate from your body until you *go!*

The most important part of this trip was the puzzle—or rather, puzzle pieces—God gave me. May I also say God is patient; He gives us whatever time we need to add another piece to His picture.

It started in Africa, on our day off. I wasn't sure how to feel—happy or guilty. Kids never get a day off from being an orphan, yet we (I) needed a break to rest and be still. God continues to show me, many times in rest. He speaks to me because I am quiet enough to listen. The life of Jesus allows us to rest in His work and work from His rest.

I enjoyed being with the group and having time away from our work. We went sightseeing, making our first stop at The World's Largest Tree, I think. It may not have been the largest, but it was exceptionally chubby. I pretended to be interested but was distracted by my thoughts. I had so many questions, so much I needed to talk to God about.

I looked out over the most beautiful land and said, "Oh God, this is not you. The land, the animals, the people—they are you. But their heartache is not you! God, you must have loved this place and these people so much for the enemy to put his stake here."

A thought came to me. "I got it, Lord!" I said. "You want us to bring You here!"

God is reclaiming Africa, I realized. I felt peace; I felt His love. Several puzzle pieces snapped into place. The words I spoke were simple, not profound at all. Yet I knew He was speaking through me to me.

I felt like a little girl. Jesus told me something so simple, but the truth of the message was as big as the parting of the Red Sea.

God wanted me to see something about the orphans. Bringing God in my heart to Africa was more than a short-term mission trip. There was more, something bigger! He was preparing me for a greater plan. I would wait and listen for His voice.

When I observe Africa, I see God's masterpiece. Everything is wonderfully overdone. I tease the Lord and say He was really showing off when He created that land.

> The land…over the top
> The animals…over the top
> The people…are the top!

I understand why the enemy wants this painting for himself. He always wants what God treasures most. I knew once again God was giving us a way to win—an opportunity, you might say—to return His treasure. How amazing! He loves us so much that He trusts us to help reclaim Africa in the name of Jesus. Doug, our global team builder, said it best: "The way I see the ministry here in Africa is the orphans are like flowers on a canvas. You need to paint them one at a time."

Pastor Doug…always available to be the hands and feet of Jesus.

You can only imagine the range of emotions I was experiencing. I knew God could reclaim Africa without us. That makes it even more amazing to me. God wants us to experience His love in us and through us. God showed me people who were harassed and helpless — sheep without a shepherd.

I looked into the eyes of the children and saw more than their pain. I saw the masterpiece God created in the beginning — I could see the image of Jesus in each one and a beauty that can overpower any evil this world can bring.

I love your people, Lord, and sometimes it hurts.

The next several days were normal — or, I might say — a different kind of normal. We were getting ready to leave for a village in Cape Town. The beauty here is as large as the devastation — miles of beautiful land and ocean, paired with miles of poverty. You can't grasp the contrast in your mind or body.

Each day, we went to an orphan drop-in center. This center is a place where the orphans can come to receive a hot meal and get help with their school work. It's meant to be a safe, comfortable place they can belong. I was blessed to see the difference Horizon International was making, and the hope it delivered to children there.

Perfectly planned, we had another day off. I don't remember much about that day off, but I remember my God Appointment with the white Afrikaner people. During our group lunch, I met a woman in the restaurant's bathroom. For some reason she was interested in me. She asked several questions, and I shared with her the details of where we were working. We both returned to our seats and carried on with lunch.

Then, God gave me a nudge to go over and talk with the woman and her group. I fought the sensation several times. After all, I was eating and enjoying a pleasant conversation with my team. Thank goodness God is persistent. The nudge became too firm to ignore. In a decision point, I excused myself and walked over to their table. "Give me the words, God," I muttered, as I often do.

"You have a wonderful wife," I said to the gentleman at the table.

"Yes, I know. I hear you are working in Kuyamandi."

"I've met some of the most wonderful people there," I replied.

"Really?" he asked. "You don't feel any danger?"

"No," I assured him. "We are there helping the orphans— we feel welcomed."

My new friend began talking about his church, and how they'd like to help or even launch a missions program but they didn't know where to start. The amazing thing is we have more connections among different races as Americans than the white Afrikaners do. I shared with him about Horizon and how they care for the orphans. Shortly after, he inquired about Horizon coming to their church to speak.

Now, I don't understand the details, but the white Afrikaners are perceived to be the people who oppress the native Africans. Much anger, hatred and prejudice has been passed down through the generations.

My heart was pounding with excitement, and I realized I was in the middle of another God Appointment. I hurried over to Bob Pearson, founder of Horizon International, who was seated at my table. Bob spoke with them, sharing from his heart and making introductions to the program's local coordinator. As we were leaving, another woman in the group asked me, "Could you come and speak at our church?"

I giggled, telling her I was a team member on a short trip and didn't work for Horizon. She patted my hand, saying, "Thank you for caring for our children."

The keyword was "our."

My next revelation was this: *How powerful would it be for the very people who are perceived as oppressors to be sent by God to help AIDS orphans!* The African people have been taught that the British and Dutch took their lives and livelihoods from them. Now the elderly are passing on from old age, the next generation is being taken by AIDS, and the children who survive will somehow come to love the Afrikaners. Another piece of the puzzle slipped into place, and a picture of forgiveness was emerging. I could hardly contain myself!

The next several days brought back my new normal—heartbreak by day, thankfulness by night. The puzzle wasn't finished, but I had what God wanted me to have. I was grateful for the picture I took home with me.

More than a year after I returned home, the images and impressions of Africa remained in my heart. I mentioned it to my children and several friends. I asked God if He wanted me to go and speak at the Afrikaner churches. (I am not at all comfortable with public speaking, but I would do it for Jesus!) I haven't heard the answers, but I am content to wait. I continue learning that my confidence cannot lay in the plan, but in God's power.

I returned to Africa in 2008 with a clear thought: *The one thing missing is having Pastor Doug speak at the local African churches.* He does so in Brazil, so it seemed appropriate that he would in Africa.

Then, two of the local African pastors asked him to preach. I don't think Pastor Doug even planned for it; it was right out of Heaven.

The service at the local churches were life-giving. The dancing and worshiping alone were more than I'd ever experienced. The message from God through Pastor Doug planted seeds of life and hope. I witnessed the progress of new friendships, relationships and, most of all, trust. Still, I didn't think about the Afrikaner churches or even my last trip's unfinished puzzle.

I went home from that trip, continuing my journey with Horizon and volunteering as an AIDS orphan advocate. In November of that year, Pastor Doug and his wife, Sandy, told me they were joining the Horizon team. Doug would train and lead teams to Africa, a perfect position for him.

The next month, on Christmas Day, I was alone with God. During this quiet time, I finally saw where each puzzle piece fit. The next piece had nothing to do with me, and I could see God's reason for the "seedtime." He had someone else in mind to reflect His image! I believe the man God has chosen to reach and teach the white Afrikaners is Pastor Doug.

Today he is preparing teams in the United States. But I believe Doug's greatest work will unfold in African and white Afrikaner churches across South Africa. I am at peace knowing God's painting is perfect and thankful it will take people from all Nations in the name of Jesus to reclaim His masterpiece.

Confirmation of this revelation came later that very day. I was at home, recovering from foot surgery. Our children were gone, visiting their in-laws for the holiday. God inspired me to ask a new friend from Zimbabwe, Patricia, to share Christmas with us.

During our evening together, I asked, "Remember Pastor Doug, who prayed for you at church? What if he could help the white Afrikaner churches build missions programs to help feed the orphans?"

Patricia's eyes filled with tears as she said, "That would be a miracle from God!"

Now, I do not know where, how or when this miracle will transpire on Earth. I do know that sometimes we plant seeds, and sometimes we water them. Only God can make them grow!

Note: I wrote this journal on December 25, 2008. On September 6, 2009, I found it under my bed; the next month God instructed me to write this book. Once again, I'm humbled by God's perfect timing! A friend once told me there is nothing passive about waiting on God. Waiting on God makes all things possible.

The true miracle of this story is how God has been waiting on me. Today is November 7, 2010. God has been giving me pieces to this puzzle for many years, and I'm not sure if this is the last piece or the first piece of a new puzzle. One thing is for sure: The pieces just keep coming.

Another piece came just a few weeks ago, as I was attending a business conference. While listening to a speaker, a thought flashed in my mind. *Go after the ones this world passes by.*

"Is this about business, Lord?" I asked.

The next day I attended a gathering to "pack and pray" for another team leaving for South Africa with Doug and Sandy. Pastor Doug said something that triggered my thoughts about the people this world has passes by. I knew God was trying to tell me something and I could hardly concentrate. I wanted more.

The next morning I received an e-mail, and there it was: an article from Pastor Doug on God's *harvest*. He said the Holy Spirit had dropped a treasure into his heart about the *harvest*. This was not just any harvest, this was *it*—the message God had been waiting so patiently for me to receive.

There is more. After writing about the harvest in *God Appointments*, I sent the draft to Theresa to review. In her e-mail, she wrote, "It needs something more." She stated that perhaps Doug will teach the Afrikaners that the *harvest* (the mission) is in their own backyard. *This moment gave God's breath away!* The situation was just like in the Bible, when

Jesus taught his disciples a new way of viewing God's plan in this world.

After reading Pastor Doug's article, it became alive in my spirit. God used this message to give me a light to see what the harvest looks like to Him. With all good intentions, I was missing God's harvest because I would invite people to church to gain knowledge about Jesus—and then wait for them to make a decision to follow Jesus. Those people would then invite more people. I thought the harvest meant increasing the numbers of healthy, interested, functioning people in the church. Of course God loves more workers, but what does God want the workers to work on?

Satan continues to tell us we need knowledge (which grows us) over obedience (which grows God). This trick is as old as Adam and Eve. At first I thought following Jesus to church was what God wanted for my life. Later I learned that Jesus is in my heart, and He is more excited about who I am *after* church.

God reveals His path through me one step at a time. First He taught me how He loves His people *through* His people. Then He revealed how to communicate through the Holy Spirit. Now God is showing me about the harvest and how to *give His breath away.*

What would happen if we invited people to work on God's harvest? In Pastor Doug's article, he wrote that the people who represent the harvest in the eye of Jesus are those who've been beaten down by the world's injustices, neglect and cruelty. They are helpless because they have no resources or advocates to help them survive and recover. (See Mathew 9:35-38.)

We can learn how to follow Jesus in church and go to heaven—or we the church can learn how to imitate Jesus as workers in His harvest field and create Heaven on Earth for all. It is not enough to tell people about Jesus. We need to allow people to experience the harvest, where all people find Jesus and God's kingdom grows for eternity.

When we wait for more workers — people with resources — to make a decision to follow Jesus, we miss the forgotten of the world who are waiting on the workers. The people who don't know Jesus are waiting to experience Jesus through the workers.

We are all waiting! The title of Pastor Doug's article said it best, "What Are We Waiting For?" We must move from waiting to working. Satan knows the harvest is great, and he makes sure the workers are few by tempting us to gain more knowledge. Authentic Kingdom Knowledge will lead us to God's harvest.

After reading Pastor Doug's article, I had to ask myself a life-changing question: *What is the knowledge of Jesus leading me to?* I have learned through experience that when we invite people to work side by side on God's harvest, we also invite the Holy Spirit to transform lives.

Let me be clear. I love going to church. I believe God wants us to gather to *worship* Him. In the love of our worship we work on His harvest. The challenge comes when people in the church do not leave the building to work on God's harvest!

Pastor Doug leaves the building, but never leaves God's people.

For me it went something like this, "Lord I did not know, but now I do. Thank you for new thoughts and your old ways."

Chapter 10

Zimbabwe and Eyes to See

One question: "Why?"
One answer: "Faith!"
One conversation: "I can see."

I woke up this morning weeping after a night of heartbreak. It's been three days since I returned from a mission trip to Zimbabwe. This morning I asked, "Why me, Lord?"

"Because you can see!"

"That is my problem, Lord!"

I can see....

I can see the man I met on the plane, who was traveling back to Africa to kill the three men who raped his sixty-one-year-old mother. I can see the African couple who has to leave their three children for months so they can earn enough money to feed them. I can see the same man who prophesied over my life. I can see the children I sponsor as they thanked me for being their new mom. I can see the son of a pastor weeping as I shared with him your Word. I can see the high school student who is desperate to be valuable to someone. I can see the girls who visited my room one by one wanting to know about your love, Lord. I can see the young woman who served us at the lodge as she sat on my bed and shared that God told her to come visit me. I can see the woman who had a dream about a white woman with long hair who would come from far away to pray that AIDS would end.

I can see the woman who was going to commit suicide — and how you trusted me to pray over her life. I can see how your Word changed her life immediately. I can see the clock that read 1:11 as I returned back to my seat. I can see the woman who sold her own child, believing she was giving her baby a chance at a better life, only to later learn the child had been murdered in a witchcraft ritual. I can see the woman who herself had murdered many children while practicing witchcraft. I can see the woman who had been abused since the age of six. I can see the woman who beat her child because the father raped her. I can see the countless AIDS orphans. I can see the tears of a fourteen-year-old girl who had not seen her mother in ten years. I can see your love in Pastor Tatenda and his wife, Lucia. I can see your forgiveness. Yes, Lord, I can see!

"Lord, I could not measure the pain. I could not measure the sin and I could not measure the beauty," I prayed. "I saw the same pain, sin and beauty in each person. It was all the same — one was not greater than the other. The pain I saw in the student who needed acceptance was the same as the pain I saw in the woman who aborted her child. I saw new life as they received your Word, Lord.

Again, I ask, 'Why me?'"

And again the Lord replied, "Because you can see!"

"Lord, I'm not sure what you are teaching me. I have no one else to ask, Lord. I have no one else to hold me. What I know for sure is that I love you and I love your people so much it hurts."

This God Appointment started when I was preparing to go to South Africa to visit orphaned children there as I had before. Our global team builder, Pastor Doug, asked if I'd be willing to go to Zimbabwe instead to present a talk and share my testimony. He shared how women in Zimbabwe were broken by their experiences with prostitution, witchcraft and AIDS and had been forgotten by the world. Those words alone should have made my decision easy. But for some reason, I couldn't receive the words and feel the compulsion to go to Zimbabwe. This was strange because usually I like to go everywhere.

So I apologized, saying over and over, "I'm *sorry*, Lord."

I knew I was being disobedient; still, I didn't want to go! A revelation came during communion several weeks later.

I bowed my head. "I am sorry, Lord. I will go."

Peace settled into my spirit, but my flesh still didn't want to go. Finally, the love from God set me free and helped me find obedience. Now I know like my next breath that satan was fearful of what God would reveal to me in Zimbabwe.

God sent me to Zimbabwe so I could experience heaven and hell on Earth. There I found the heart of God and His son, Jesus, who died for His Father's heart (us).

The decision point that changed my life—and the reason God sent me to Zimbabwe—arrived as I was listening to a Zimbabwean woman share her testimony with the group. She spoke of how she was abandoned as a child only to be controlled by an older man who practiced witchcraft and raped her repeatedly from age three. Much of her story I blanked out of my mind, but I remember what she did to young, innocent babies.

She explained how she would pose as a midwife, drug pregnant women, take the newborn babies and tell the mothers their babies died at birth. She went on to explain—through screams, gasps and sobs—that she then decapitated the children and sold their heads to those who practiced witchcraft. Somewhere in this life of horror, she found her way to Jesus.

Hearing her testimony was like nothing I had ever experienced. Her words spoke such death, yet her eyes were filled with life. As she finished speaking, I walked out on the stage and took her hand while she wept.

I was moved to hug her. "Your sin is no greater than mine," I whispered to her.

The words came out of my mouth, but they didn't feel like they were mine. At the time I didn't realize the magnitude of what I'd said. When I arrived home later, God spoke to my heart. I wondered how could she have done such a thing—

and how my own hands had touched the hands of a woman who had butchered babies.

Just a few days after that encounter, I received the revelation that would change my life forever. It came like a flash in my head.

She did not speak English! Her testimony had been translated, so she could not have understood my words to her.

Immediately I realized the message I spoke was for me. Her sin really was no greater than mine, though I had never murdered a child. I was one with her in Christ for better or for worse. *This moment gave God's breath away.*

In Zimbabwe God taught me the depth of His love. He showed me that His grace has no boundaries for those who believe. He taught me that we do become a new creation in Him. Despite her horrible sins, the woman I heard and hugged was beautiful and courageous, and Jesus was visible in her eyes.

How could I have been reluctant to go? How many children murdered or dying from AIDS would it take for me to stop and take notice? The answer should be only one child!

We tend to be victims of statistics. When we hear the overwhelming numbers, we may feel there is no hope.

For years I chose to do nothing. Finally I wondered, *Where was I when the number was* one *child?* The enemy tells me I can make no difference now. God tells me differently—that the number is always one.

The Lord revealed His heart to me as He took my pain away. And I understood that we were never meant to measure each other's sin, pain or beauty. We can never compare whose is greater. I believe that God sees but does not measure. All measurement died with Jesus on the cross. The gift He gives now is love, hope and faith—the only way burdens can be taken away. Many times through love, we need to have and give hope first, so His people can have faith in *something*.

Now I realize my fear in going to Zimbabwe was because I didn't want to stand in front of people and tell my real testimony. *With all of the pain, suffering and true horror these woman had been through, what I could bring?* Parts of my past were difficult, but nothing I experienced could compare to their stories.

What a privilege to share love, hope,
and faith with sisters in Christ.

To my surprise, my life experience was exactly what they needed to hear. Many of the Zimbabwean women thought bad things happened to them because they were black. My story helped them understand that the enemy wants to take all of us down, and that the color of our skin is beautiful because God created each of us. Together we are the perfect color for His Kingdom.

Before my trip I said, "Lord, I have no talent."

He said, "Good. I have talent!"

I said, "Lord, I am shy."

He said, "I am bold!"

I said, "Lord, I am not smart."

He said, "I have the wisdom of My Father!"

I said, "Lord, I was going to kill my child."

He said, "I know. My Father gave my life for love!"

I said, "Lord, I can't."

He said, "I can!"

I said, "Lord, I didn't want to go to Zimbabwe."

He said, "I know. You went for me!"

This morning the truth set me free. Sin, pain and beauty are true to each of us, but none of them is The Truth.

Many times I've told myself I have no right to feel pain when people have it so much worse. I've learned that each life — including every bit of sin, pain and beauty — is important to Jesus. He sees all, but what He *measures* is faith. Faith pleases God; Faith moves God. We need to see sin, pain and beauty only to know they are powerful to the beholder and give us opportunity to introduce love, hope and faith. When we measure we lose; when we see He saves.

A conversation with God saved my life again. I will spend my time differently today and tomorrow. I will never forget Zimbabwe or its people. I am safe at home, and I have the choice to serve God's people. Being here may not seem as important as going to Zimbabwe, but to God there is no measurement — just love, hope and faith!

I am thankful for the life Jesus has given me. I will go wherever He sends me next, not because I am ready or worthy, but because I am willing.

In the beginning of this story, I asked, "Why me?" I should have asked, "Why *not* me?" If God can use me, He can use anyone.

If we join together, we can each help one child and make, "One for the family" our common bond. If you can help one, please visit www.horizoninternationalinc.com or link to Horizon International through www.godappointments.com.

Creating a world of Hope for AIDS orphans in Africa, one child at a time.

A life is always good.

Chapter 11

Keontaye and the Girl Who Jumped

I remember this warm summer day because God let me watch someone I love experience a life-changing God Appointment.

My husband, Brian, and I were on our way home from dinner out with our family. We were a few blocks away from our daughter Billie's home when we saw two police officers at the side of the road. Getting closer, Billie noticed the officers were poised over a boy on the ground. She recognized him as one of the foster kids who lived down the road.

"I know that kid!" she yelled, leaping out of our Suburban. Mind you, Billie has always been our calm, reserved child. As a young adult, she continues to be ladylike, collected and appropriate at all times.

Without thinking, I was out of the car right behind her. In amazement I watched as Billie questioned the officers and then crouched on the ground next to the boy.

His name, Billie later told me, was Keontaye. A big black kid, Keontaye was just twelve but he was built like a sixteen-year-old. His face was wet with sweat, drool and tears.

In my memory I can still see my daughter rubbing Keontaye's back as she assured him he wouldn't be hurt.

Loving but firm, she told the boy to be respectful and calm down. He trusted her immediately, listening to every word.

I'd never experienced anything so natural in my life. My daughter was giving a gift that could come only from God.

As we got back in the car, Billie didn't take her eyes off Keontaye. She had tears as we drove away, and I couldn't help but be concerned for what my daughter might be getting into.

A few days later, Billie told me Keontaye had come by her house with a message.

"Mom, Keontaye gave me a note with his caseworker's number, just in case I ever wanted to adopt him."

I giggled, not entirely sure how to respond. God was up to something — but that *something* was between Billie and God.

Within the week, Billie canceled a weekend trip with our family so she could apply for a foster care license. I listened to her plans but didn't ask many questions about Keontaye or her intentions.

As mothers, we want to protect our children — no matter how old they grow. I knew how hard Billie worked; I knew she had other life struggles she was working through. *Could she handle one more thing?*

This time, she showed me how God provides strength to achieve the tasks that are important to Him.

I'm going to jump ahead and tell you that Billie did get her foster care license, which resulted in a wealth of beautiful stories and struggles that could be shared in another book.

As for Keontaye, his life hasn't been easy. He stayed with Billie on most weekends and many weeknights. But before he came into our family, he witnessed and experienced things no child should have to. At times Billie no doubt wanted to give up. In those difficult moments she would say, "I know God gave him to me."

As a foster parent, Billie could have taken the easy route by coddling Keontaye and trying to fix his problems for him. But she didn't take pity on him or relax her high standards because of his difficult past. In this and other ways, Billie was the perfect player in this God Appointment. She is loving and gentle, yet she makes all of her kids toe the line. And Keontaye accepts her authority because he knows it comes from a place of love. Ephesians 4:15 says, *"Instead, speaking the truth in love, we will in all things grow up into him who is the Head, that is, Christ."*

Today as I'm writing this book Keontaye is sixteen years old. He is a treasure to our family, and we cannot imagine life without him. But all of God's children—the ones we give birth to and the ones we don't—are on loan to us. And that includes Keontaye.

Billie's hope from the day she met Keontaye was that one day a good family would adopt him. Yet she didn't realize how much she would grow to love him and consider him a true part of the family.

And so she had mixed emotions when a woman named Dawn approached Billie at church and asked about Keontaye. She explained that she and her husband, Bill, were hoping to adopt a child.

Hearing this, Billie burst into tears. She knew this was the answer to her prayers, yet she felt her heart was being ripped from her chest. She wasn't sure what to think—or whether she even *wanted* to think. The situation was something only God could handle, so Billie decided to give Keontaye back to Him and wait for the next step.

When God's plan is in place and each participant is obedient, the most amazing miracles happen. Our family had gone to the same church for more than twenty years when God called us to attend another church in our community. There was nothing wrong with our original church; we have many friends and family members who worship there. The point is that God directed us to go, so we did. Many times I thought the change *must* be God's doing because it's unlike us to pick up and move. As each member of our family attended the new church, the comment was the same: "It just seems right."

Meanwhile another family was praying for God's direction. Bill and Dawn, both members of our new church, are wonderful people with four grown children and two grand-children. From the time their own children were small, they felt God calling them to adopt. As the years passed and they raised their family, that desire never went away. Eventually, they shared this longing with their prayer group and began exploring their options. They attended classes about adoption at our church to prepare for what they thought God wanted for them.

Their own plan had always been to adopt an Asian girl. Dawn had raised three girls and was equipped and excited to raise another one. During her prayers, Dawn thanked God for putting adoption on her heart and for the little girl He would bring to their family. But most of all, she prayed that God would bring them the child He wanted them to have.

Through her prayers, Dawn was amazed to discover that God was showing her something—or *someone*—very different from the one she had always envisioned. This one was much bigger, much older and much darker. To top it off, the child was an African-American boy, not an Asian girl.

God was working all the while to bring Dawn and Bill exactly what they prayed for. And the beautiful thing is that they gave away their own personal plan to fulfill God's plan. In faith they accepted God's will and received the love God brings only through obedience.

One day during this season of prayer, Dawn received a book from the foster care system, seemingly "out of the blue." As she flipped through the pages, she stopped at a photo of Keontaye. Something made her pause.

When I met Dawn the first time, I asked her why the photo stood out. "It was his smile," she replied. *This moment gave God's breath away.* Then I looked at Keontaye, smiled and gave him a high five. You see, when Billie first met him, he didn't smile much. So Billie would encourage him, commenting on how handsome he looked when he grinned.

Dawn's comment made me realize this puzzle was made by God, but He wanted all of us to have the experience of laying each piece down together—one by one.

Dawn then shared her side of story, explaining how she was watching an online video of Keontaye when Bill recognized him as "the kid who went with the white girl to church." Dawn felt more drawn to the boy, but still wasn't sure he was the one. So she prayed, "Lord, I always wanted a little Asian girl, but this is not about what I want. It's about what *You* want."

God's answer was clear. He showed her Keontaye's face and said by the Holy Spirit, "that one." From then, Dawn didn't question that God intended for Keontaye to be her son. The very next Sunday Dawn approached Billie at church.

For her part, Billie knew in faith that this was the family she'd been praying for. This was the family she could give Keontaye to. Families in the past had inquired, but Billie was not peaceful and had prayed against it. At times, I thought she wouldn't give him up and no family would be good enough.

I must admit that I prayed to God that no one would take Keontaye far away from us. I also knew that God hadn't convicted Billie to adopt him herself—and now I knew why. I don't usually ask for specific things in my prayers because I'm so limited in what I want and think. But my prayer for Keontaye was different: "Please, Lord, don't take him far away. I don't think my daughter could take it."

To be truthful, I didn't think *I* could take it. I worried not only about the pain of my own heart, but also the pain of Billie, her kids Devon, Andres and Lenox. Not to mention the pain of my daughter Robbie Sue, her husband, Will, and their kids, Dayton and Corbin. The whole family had fallen in love with Keontaye.

Billie and Dawn began talking regularly. They discovered similarities in many ways. God knew it would take a special person for Billie to let Keontaye go—or rather, to share him with.

Indeed, Dawn and Bill are among the most amazing people I've ever met. You can see it in their children and grandchildren. You can see it in the way they share Keontaye with us. They want what's best in and for his life.

Yet even with all of the blessings, my daughter has struggled through this transition. She has had many days of tears and pain. But I admire how Billie has been obedient to God's will, as she says in a gentle, sweet voice, "Bill and Dawn's family is the best thing that could ever happen for Keontaye."

God comes to make a way, not to take away!

God's plan always grows the Kingdom. Our family grew because we chose to grow the Kingdom family. Bill and Dawn's family is becoming part of our family, and we will become part of their family. We are all Keontaye's family.

When Keontaye was born, God knew his parents would give him and his three sisters away. He was with his parents until he was five years old, many years of "seed time"—time spent waiting on the Lord and preparing to live out His plan—that no one will ever understand. What I do know is this child and his three little sisters are valuable to God. God placed the sisters with a family right away and saved Keontaye for us. In fact, he waited *11 years* for his new family.

This God Appointment has been a blessing to experience, greater than words can express. I watched my family embrace someone no one else wanted—not because he wasn't worthy or valuable, because God was saving him "for such a time as this."

We recently celebrated Keontaye's sixteenth birthday with a surprise party at his new home. With all of our families together, Dawn and I discovered that our daughters even look alike! There are no limits to God's goodness when we choose to receive it.

In this God Appointment, I got to watch two families come together to become one family in Christ!

One more thing…. If you ever meet Keontaye, be sure to see his smile. It's worth a thousand words!

*Billie and Keontaye... when love is big enough
the facts don't count.*

Chapter 12

The Power of Prayer–Even When It Is Not Your Own

On January 4, 2010, I woke up feeling uneasy, like something was wrong. I was restless and knew I had to find peace so God could direct me.

The uncertainty, I later realized, came from the tentative steps I was taking. The steps weren't wrong, but they didn't line up with the direction God was sending me.

Many times I've chosen not to do something good because I didn't feel God's call to action. God is pleased when He directs us and we follow, the same way parents are blessed when children obey. Yet it's also gratifying when kids do good things on their own, when we don't push, coach, cajole or yell at them to do it. I delight when my grown children do God's work without any help from me.

The Bible is full of direction. We can gain knowledge to do His work, which delights Him. Where we need to be cautious is when *our* work for Him comes before *His* work for Him. I'm talking about when the Holy Spirit speaks to us, and we're too busy doing good things that we don't hear His voice.

This is why I am writing today. I'm not going to blame it on the enemy — we give him too much credit. When we do something wrong, we tend to blame our activities on the enemy instead of taking responsibility for our choices. Sometimes we just mess up even when our heart is in the right place.

One year after my first trip to Zimbabwe, I felt grateful, even indebted to the lessons I learned there. The message was powerful, giving me a better, lasting understanding of God's deep love. I resisted going on this trip and spent weeks struggling and fabricating every variety of excuse. When I made the decision to go last year, I felt fear in my flesh even though my spirit was at peace. I have grown "addicted" to the peace only the Lord can bring.

The women's conference in Zimbabwe was life-changing for me. Even before it concluded, I was planning to return for the next one in April 2010. I didn't pray about the decision but assumed God would want me to go again because of my experience the first time. This time, my heart was in the right place but I didn't leaving room for God's heart. And I've learned that if I want God's best, I have to listen for His voice.

Throughout the year as I shared what God had taught me, I would confirm my attendance at next year's conference. Again, I don't think I was doing anything wrong. If God didn't have other plans for me, He would be blessed by my decision to go to Zimbabwe. But with prayer, God communicates through the Holy Spirit to give us His best. Without the Holy Spirit, we can miss the messages that come straight from God.

This background explains why I woke up restless that January morning. The deadline to register for the Zimbabwe conference was near. A year had passed since the last trip. The deposit and application were due and I had already verbally committed to going. Many good friends were going.

I tried to blame my unease on fleshly things, not dreaming it was God nudging me. Why I didn't pray for guidance, I don't know.

I just assumed God wanted me to go to Zimbabwe! Through prayer I found peace, and in that peace God revealed His plan for me to go to South Africa instead. It turns out that the prayer in question wasn't my own. It was the prayer of a friend who interceded for me. When I was weak, God used a friend's strength to deliver the peace and quiet I needed to listen. I then could recognize that the enemy wasn't stopping me from going — it was *me* not leaving room for the Holy Spirit to direct me. I assumed I was doing the right thing and God would want me to fight the battle the same way as before.

That morning in my discomfort, I didn't do my devotions. I arrived at work more frustrated. A friend called and I shared my thoughts about Zimbabwe and what I thought was the reason for my restlessness. He didn't offer me advice — which was even more frustrating — but he did offer prayer. But even as he prayed, I was preoccupied. I didn't receive all the words, but I felt peace wash over me.

After the call, I continued responding to e-mails and preparing sales reports. I spoke with another friend, and during our conversation she mentioned that my daughter Billie said God had put it on her heart to go to Africa. Billie and I had always talked about going to South Africa when her kids were older. Again, I went on with my day.

But God was putting the pieces together, waiting for me to be at peace so I could receive His voice through the Holy Spirit.

Later that day, I thought about the South Africa youth trip and wondered who would lead the contingent of young girls. A female chaperone always goes along to advocate and watch over the girls. I made some calls and found the position hadn't been filled. Then came a call from another friend, who said he'd been thinking about Billie going to South Africa. I couldn't believe it! I felt an excitement and total peacefulness that can only come from God.

"God, is this what you want me to do?" I asked.

I called Billie Lou to tell her about my day and what God was calling us to do. When I asked if she needed to pray about it, she replied, "No, I'm fine. I already knew I was going." She proceeded to tell me she'd already scheduled time off of work to go to South Africa.

My daughter, Billie, was the answer to prayer.

When you hear God's voice through the Holy Spirit, what you are committed to here on Earth doesn't matter. There is nothing above intimacy with God. This connection breeds passion, and passion brings purpose. Passion and purpose together can move mountains. *This moment gave God's breath away.*

I was doing what God wanted, overwhelmed with excitement and energy to work for Him. I started the next morning with my devotion and even read the devotions I missed. Turns out, the devotion for January 4 would have been helpful. It read: "All is well. Wonderful things are happening. Do not limit God at all. He cares and provides. Uproot self—you are the channel blocker. Do not plan ahead; the way will unfold step by step. Leave tomorrow's burden. Christ is the great Burden bearer. You cannot bear His load and He only expects you to carry a little day share."

From *God Calling*, published by Barbour Publishing, Inc.
Used by permission.

My heart filled with joy; my thoughts ran wild with possibilities. Several spots on the mission team were still open, and I prayed for God to choose them, saying "Lord, you know the team. Bring them to me, and I will serve them."

I called my mom and attempted to explain what had happened. Of course, the details never sound as amazing to others as it does to the one *accepting* God's direction. Nevertheless, she was pleased. Within several hours I spoke with my sister, Lisa. She too prays in the Spirit and is attuned to God's voice.

She said, "I heard you and Billie are joining a team of young people to South Africa." Her next words were that she believed God was leading her to send her children, Hunter and Coleton.

Out of the blue, I e-mailed my friend, Suzanna, to have lunch. As I was sharing the story of my impending trip, we both had thoughts of her son, Alex, and concluded this lunch was God's invitation for him to go. The situation was unfolding like a dream, and God was telling me when and where. On my way back to work, I kept thinking of other kids I knew. I called their parents as fast as the thoughts came.

There were roadblocks, of course. I've learned to invite road blocks as opportunities to exercise faith. Faith moves God like nothing else.

Later that day my sister Lisa called back. She'd been saving money she'd received for Christmas. Though the family had been hit hard by the recession and they needed the money to pay bills, the total would cover the down payment for her two children. Through the Spirit, God made a way.

Faith moves God, and He continues to give us more than we ask for. Though content with my direction, God gave me more confirmation at my Wednesday night Bible study. The lesson was on David—how before each battle he prayed to God. He never assumed God would want him to fight each battle the same way. Our pastor, Tavio, taught us that we occasionally need someone to hold up our tired arms, the same way men helped hold up Moses' arms during battle. Tears flowed at the thought that God cared enough not only to wait on me, but to help me understand His heart through confirmation.

Of course, the story continues. The ending will never come here on earth, because God's best plan is after we leave this world. I have found Heaven on Earth through my God Appointments.

I later received a call from a woman named Silvana. I didn't know who she was until she explained that a friend of hers had met me in Africa the year before. She had been wanting to travel to Africa and soon committed to joining us on this trip as well. (You'll read more about Silvana in "Currency Exchange.")

In faith many things have to happen to complete the mission for God—things like passports, finances, attitudes, parental approval and, most of all, the process of "keeping the faith." But we shouldn't worry, because the battle already is won. On the journey, we get to see and enjoy the evidence of God's victory. Enjoy the ride!

Chapter 13

Currency Exchange

M oney to God is nothing more than a bartering tool. Its value goes up and down — but the true value is what you get in return. Some people collect treasures; some people collect trash. The value of either one is in the eye of the beholder.

I have been accused of not appreciating the value of money. I've just never worried about how much I have, what it can buy or the security it brings. How badly I want something determines its value to me, and the actual cost doesn't matter. Now, you may be thinking money matters if you *don't* have it. But I find that if God puts something on my heart, it probably won't be about my money. More likely, it was my limited thinking that kept me from moving ahead in God's plan.

Two years before my father died, I was spending time with him over the Fourth of July weekend. We were at my parent's tranquil summer home in Michigan. The two of us had a wonderful tradition of sitting on the back porch gazing out over Lake Michigan and talking about life. On this occasion we discussed work, and I told my dad how much I appreciated all the years he'd worked hard to support and provide for our family. My next question — or rather, his next answer — gave new meaning to my life.

"Daddy, when do I slow down?" I asked.

"Bobbie, not until every child is fed," he replied.

To this point I'd never gone on a mission trip or even thought about feeding kids. I hadn't come to see myself as God sees me, and I didn't yet know who I really was in Christ. Yet I could sense that my dad was planting this seed in my heart. And as I discovered the process of learning to trust, that seed was allowed to grow.

Years later—in November 2009— I was walking through the airport in Johannesburg, South Africa. I'd spent a beautiful week working with AIDS orphans and thought nothing could change my upbeat mood. But then one of my team members said something that hurt my feelings, and I stormed off.

Have you ever behaved in a way that instantly made you want to crawl in a hole and hide? That was me in that moment. In my heart, I probably was more emotional about leaving than I wanted to admit. (If you're a woman, you already understand how emotions and feelings can be harmful to your life; if you're a man, you too understand how a woman's emotions and feelings can be harmful to your life.)

As I rounded a corner in the airport, I spotted a sign that read, "Currency Exchange." This kiosk provided the perfect place for me to hide for a moment and exchange my leftover money. Standing in line, I noticed a man next to me. He was being told his credit card wouldn't work, and he wouldn't be able to get the money he needed. I looked down at the bills and coins in my hand. Oddly enough, the cash added up to the exact amount he was asking for. God instantly put it on my heart to hand over my money to this stranger.

Everyone who knows me understands that I'm not the most sophisticated person. I sometimes blurt out things that I'm immediately sorry for. But I do the same thing for God, and God is good all of the time. My decision to obey God at the currency exchange began a never-ending God Appointment— one that reminds me of money. As money flows through our lives, we know very little about where it came from and what it has been used for. As Pastor Doug always says, "We are on a no-need-to-know basis."

Looking at the man next to me, I said, "I have that exact amount, and I want you to have it."

He didn't want to take it, so I explained that God had compelled me to give it to him. He introduced himself as Andre and thanked me.

I walked away, remembering my earlier misbehavior with my friend and feeling ashamed all over again. So I shuffled into a store across the way to waste a little more time. I grabbed some water and a snack for the plane ride home. In the checkout line, a distinguished businessman stood in front of me. The cashier had tried to process his credit card, but the transaction wouldn't go through. Once again, the Lord urged me to pay for his stuff. The total came to the equivalent of seventy-five American dollars. By now I thought it would have been easier (and cheaper) to apologize to my teammate and go to the departure gate. The man had no South African rand, but he offered to reimburse me in euros. I didn't want to accept the money, but he insisted, so I stuffed in the bills in my wallet and forgot about it. I didn't even know how much the currency was worth. Walking at last to the gate, I dwelled on the ways God uses me even when I'm exceptionally cranky.

Back at the gate, I couldn't find any of my teammates. I'd been practicing my apology, but God had other plans. There at the gate was Andre, the gentleman from the currency exchange. He told me I was an answer to prayer, and a friend of his had needed the money. He just wanted to thank me again. Then he added that he wanted me to take his plane seat in first class. I thanked him but said that I needed to stay with my mission team. He began asking questions about what we were doing in Africa, which gave me the opportunity to tell Andre about Horizon International and our work to help AIDS orphans.

Andre said he had a friend, Silvana, who had always wanted to spend time in Africa. She had planned to do mission work with a friend, but that friend had sadly died before they'd been able to. Andre asked for my business card to take to Silvana. "I know I met you for a reason, and I know that God brought us together," he said.

About that time, my friend walked up and I introduced him to Andre. I was so joyous over this God Appointment that I forgot how immature I'd acted earlier. They too talked and exchanged business cards. I found out later that Andre worked for the U.S. government and frequently visited embassies in Africa.

I arrived safely home from Africa, and several months later I took a business trip to San Antonio, Texas. I stayed with my friend Jane, who comes from a long line of people who worship Jesus. Spending time with her always leaves me feeling renewed.

On my way home, I had several hours to wait at the airport before my connecting flight departed from Houston. I felt peaceful and enjoyed my time with little to do but wait.

At an airport restaurant, I noticed that all of the patrons but me seemed foreign. "I feel like I'm in the international wing," I laughed. Sure enough, every flight in that corridor was going to a faraway destination. Looking at all of the beautiful, unique faces, I said over and over, "I love your people, Lord." I felt the depth of His love for each one.

My words pumped the life of His Spirit into my flesh. I made eye contact with each person, as if we knew each other and could see more than our shells. The connection was spiritual, and I felt each person knew what I knew about God. One woman was in a wheelchair, her head curled toward her lap. As I stared at the top of her head, she raised her face just long enough to meet my eyes. I stopped as she rolled by to embrace the encounter.

I snapped out of the moment when I looked up to spot a **currency exchange** stand. The sign jogged my memory of the Euros I'd been carrying around since I returned from Africa. Low on cash, I decided to exchange the foreign money, which I thought to be worth about seventy-five American dollars.

The young girl in line ahead of me, probably a student, had a European accent of some kind. Her body language told me she was sad. She was trying to exchange her money and told the woman she needed seventy-five American dollars. She was clearly struggling as she counted her pennies. My next thought, straight from the Lord, went something like this: "Give her the Euros." My own wallet was running on empty, and so I stalled a little, making excuses.

But before I knew it, I heard myself say, "Here, I want to give you this money."

"No, thank you!" she replied with obvious pride.

The lady at the kiosk chimed in. "If you try to exchange it, it will be too complicated."

"I don't want to exchange it," I said. "I want to give it to her."

"No," the girl repeated, seemingly skeptical of my motives and trying to keep me out of her private matter.

I tried again. "You don't understand. The Lord told me to give this to you."

Right away, the worker said to the girl, "Ma'am, you have to take it because if God is telling her to give it to you, you don't want to stand between her and God."

The girl looked at both of us with clear confusion. She let down her guard long enough to stick out her hand and take the money. I'll never forget her face; she was so puzzled that all I could do was give her a hug and wish her good day. I walked out feeling like a million bucks. I was another seventy-five dollars in the hole and had never felt better. When God barters, the money does not matter.

Walking toward my gate I continued to say, "I love your people, Lord." I couldn't stop smiling, even as I felt everyone was looking at me.

When it was nearly boarding time, I noticed a really tall man staring at me—not in a flirtatious way but with a puzzled expression. I had attended Oak Hills Church that morning, where Max Lucado preachers and many San Antonio Spurs basketball players worship. This man was as tall as any basketball player, so I wondered if I'd seen him in church. I avoided his gaze and boarded the plane at my first chance.

At the airport in Indianapolis, my bags failed to arrive at the baggage claim. All of the other passengers on my flight had gone, and I couldn't reach the shuttle to the parking lot to ask the driver to wait. By the time my bags finally showed up, I knew the shuttle bus would be gone. I resigned myself for a long wait for the next one. Out in the cold at the bus stop, I saw a shuttle van and another passenger — the tall man from the Houston airport.

"It's you," I blurted.

"I know, I was thinking the same thing," he said, clearly puzzled.

He apologized right away for staring at me, but he explained that I had been glowing when he saw me. I told him about my spiritual experience at the airport, and how I'd been studying faith. He replied that he'd been studying the substance of faith. As I listened, I knew this encounter was another God Appointment.

He said he worked for Shell Oil Company and had started a Bible study in the workplace — against his boss' wishes. He figured that if God was for him, who dare be against him. I became his student as I listened to his words. He was writing a book, and he wanted me to know that God brought us together.

He told me that a few minutes before I showed up for the shuttle, the driver asked him if he was willing to wait for the remaining passenger. He was tired and had a long drive, but agreed to wait. He admitted that he'd really thought, *No, I don't want to wait any longer.* I believe that he waited because he made himself available to God. While I'd been studying faith, God wanted me to learn more. He wanted me to know that sometimes the substance of faith — the things we cannot see — becomes more real than things we can see with our natural eyes. Substance is what we know is true even before it manifests.

I am blessed to meet God's people while I continue to live my life. As I left the airport parking lot, I thought, *How does*

God know exactly what I need each step of the way? I thanked God for this gift and drove home.

The hardest part of my life is trying to explain my days to the people I love. So many God Appointments I can't share simply because I don't know where to start. The simplest ones seem to be the appointments God is able to do the most with. Some of the ones I'm sharing in this book may seem big, and yet the small ones mean just as much to God and to me.

In another chapter I wrote about how I was preparing to go to Zimbabwe when God called me to South Africa. From the moment I decided to go, God began building the mission team. Three days after I made my decision to go, I received a call from Silvana, the friend of Andre, whom I'd met at the currency exchange in South Africa. Silvana called to tell me she was ready to go on a mission trip. The minute I heard her voice, I knew God was sending her to me. She explained that she had no money and wasn't sure how the trip would happen, but she knew she was supposed to go with me. Andre hadn't stopped talking about our meeting at the airport, she told me, and he too believed she was meant to go to Africa with our team.

Silvana brought more than herself; she came to give God's breath away.

Two weeks before the trip was scheduled to depart, Silvana arrived from Yonkers, New York, to meet the students and the rest of our team. We spent an entire day together. I was taken back by her love for God's people and her vision to bring missions programs to the churches in New York City. She said the churches were filled with beautiful people who would love to help. And after spending time with Silvana in Africa, I fully believe she will bless New York by allowing God to love His people and orphans through them. She is a bright light for God! I will never get used to the depth of God's love for all of his people and the way He chose us to shine His light.

By the way, that mission team included *11* American students who hosted a retreat for teenaged AIDS orphans. My favorite gift was watching these students transform as they discovered their purpose. Pastor Doug has often said that today's kids don't need pity, they need purpose. In Africa I experienced this with my own eyes. When the students had orphans to care for, they transformed into new creations. Even their outward appearances changed.

After the trip, the questions parents asked most frequently was, "How do we keep a purpose in front of our children?" My initial answer was that we need to teach them—and reteach them—how much God loves each of them. But I knew something was missing in my words, so I called Pastor Doug.

"It is more than just knowing God loves us," Doug said. "Kids today are taught that the world and God owe them something. They need to know it's not about having a great life. It's about living a life of greatness for God."

He went on to explain that kids need to learn how to let God love people through them.

"Students need to see the people here in the United States like they see the orphans in Africa," he explained.

When the students cared for the orphans, they became servers and learners. When they are at home, they want to be served.

Something else Doug said was that "kids need to be the answer, not the problem."

His vision for "teen answers" — not *teenagers* — has shown me that students (in fact, all people) want to be the answer. When we allow God to love others through us, many times we become an answer to prayer.

People all over the world — like Silvana, like me, like you, like modern American teenagers — are waiting to be used by God. Each of us was created with a desire to love God and let God's love flow through us to others. Many young people are sad and lonely because they long for a purpose bigger than themselves. I don't know all of the answers and many times I don't even know the questions, but what I do know is God's love heals and takes us places we never thought we could go.

When I was back at the airport to leave for South Africa, I decided to stop at the currency exchange kiosk in Indianapolis. I wasn't thinking about another God Appointment. I simply wanted to change my money. When I stepped up to the window, the lady helping me said, "Where are you going?"

She laughed when I said "South Africa," explaining that she'd been praying to go there. Also a teacher, she had been saving books for years with the intention of giving them to AIDS orphans. When she said God had sent me to her window, all I could say is, "I know He did." I gave her my phone number and said I looked forward to being her friend.

Having Jesus in our lives allows us to celebrate every day. The love, favor, kindness and peace we receive to give others are beyond anything else we could hope for.

Likewise, serving Jesus is a privilege and honor. This God Appointment will never be over, because the seeds planted will grow around the world.

Someday, every child will be fed. I don't have to see it; I just have to believe in faith. This sounds like an opportunity for *substance....*

Chapter 14

God or Gun?

I thought my trip to Zimbabwe would be my one and only experience of heaven and hell on earth. Now I know that God used my Zimbabwe trip to prepare me for the future.

As long as I can remember, He has blessed me with God Appointments. I pray each morning that He'll bring people into my life who need to hear His words — and He does. Time after time, I am honored to love His people. I leave each one thinking, *Thank you, Lord.*

I learned today that opportunity lies in the uncomfortable. It's easy to do things we like to do. It's easy to love people who are loveable. It's easy to go where we want to go. At the end of the day, we choose to do what is comfortable for us.

One Saturday during Labor Day weekend, my alarm went off at 5:15 a.m. like it does every morning. I put on my sweats and started in on my stretches. All the while I was reflecting on First Corinthians, the chapter of the Bible that deals most notably with love. I prayed extra long that morning and had wonderful thoughts about how I love God's people.

As I left to meet my husband for breakfast, I remembered that I needed to take a package to our foster grandson, Keontaye, for a youth retreat. I stopped by the gas station and noticed a young woman with bruises on the side of her face. I'd seen these kinds of bruises before and knew from experience exactly what they were. Normally I would have bad thoughts about the person who inflicted them. Today was different. The moment I saw this woman, I determined that she is the fruit, so I must pray for the root—the person who hurt her.

This was new for me. My heart is kind and forgiving, but I don't recall focusing love on the abuser before. I thanked God for showing me a new level of love. Little did I know He was preparing me for my next God Appointment.

I met Brian at our favorite breakfast place. Brian likes the food; I love the people who work there. Over the last year, I'd become aware of one of the waiters. A Hispanic man in his late twenties, he would clear everyone's table but never came close to ours or tried to make eye contact with us. His stand-offishness was a stark contrast to the other workers at the restaurant, who were friendly and welcoming. My heart felt sad for him. I made a point to glance his way, but he never looked up at me. I sensed he was hiding something, maybe pain.

This morning was different. As he was walking by our table, I looked up and caught his gaze. He stopped and then looked at my Bible on the table.

"Is that a Bible?" he asked.

"Yes," I said. "Do you know about the Bible?"

I think he muttered, "yes and no." He introduced himself as Gabe and explained that he'd attended seminary, but hadn't gone to church for four years. I told him not to worry because church was still in his heart. He asked me where I worshipped.

"Several places," I replied. "Would you like to come with us sometime?"

When he said he worked on Sundays, I asked him to join us on a Saturday night. He didn't commit, but he did ask for our phone numbers.

I was so excited! Brian was laughing because I couldn't stop smiling and saying, "Thank you," Jesus."

Brian and I parted, and I got into my car. I'm usually quiet when I worship, but today I couldn't contain myself.

Much to my surprise, I even began shouting in the Spirit. (I think I scared myself!) God was getting me ready for my next appointment.

I drove to a parking lot to pray quietly. My phone rang; it was Gabe from the restaurant. He asked me to meet him at 3:00 p.m. when his shift ended.

I agreed, and as I hung up I said, "Thank you, Jesus, for my life. I *love* your people."

I went to my grandson Andreas' football game, then left at halftime for my appointment with Gabe. I called Brian on the way to tell him the great news.

I arrived right at 3:00 p.m. and pulled my Bible out of my purse. I assumed I'd be looking up scripture and telling him at length about God's love.

I watched Gabe leave the building and put his coat on. This struck me as strange because it was 81 degrees. I unlocked the passenger door and let him in. Immediately, I noticed he seemed different and was very fidgety.

"I want to tell you everything so you understand," he said.

First he told me that he had watched me for the last year. He couldn't come by me, he explained, because of my spirit. He said he sensed a strong peace around me and knew what it was.

For the next hour and a half, Gabe told me his life story. He began with the day he was visiting his aunt and uncle, and a woman came to the door to tell them about Jesus. He was young at the time but he sensed the same peace around her that he had with me. He listened as the woman explained the Gospel to his family members, but he told himself it wasn't his business. Still, he didn't forget the woman's words.

When Gabe was seventeen, a friend invited him to church. When he entered the church, he felt a peace like never before.

From what I could gather, Gabe's life had been full of heartache and disappointment. When he went home after church, he did not feel peace. He wanted to feel like that again but didn't know how.

The next time he visited the church, he took a Bible home with him, thinking it would help him experience the same peace at home. But it didn't. He took his family with him to church, thinking this would help him feel peaceful at home. But it didn't happen.

A friend told Gabe that Jesus died so he could be forgiving and if he believes, Jesus would be the peace in his life. That day, Gabe accepted Jesus and finally was able to take the peace home with him in his spirit.

Somehow, he found out about a seminary program. He was told it would take four years, lots of money and much sacrifice. Yet he wanted to attend more than anything else in his life. He worked long hours, first to save up for his schooling and then to do well in his classes. When old friends noticed that he was serious about seminary, they started to threaten him and his family. They recognized that Gabe was intent on serving the Lord and were determined to keep him from it. These same people also were influencing Gabe's brother-in-law to keep him from going to school.

I've since forgotten many details of Gabe's story because it was painful for him to speak and painful for me to hear. But I remember Gabe telling me that his foes would take his written papers and burn them. They even attacked Gabe's father in front of him, breaking his arms and asking, "Are you going to fight now?" Gabe did nothing because he was determined to show them God's forgiveness.

So they raped his mother in front of him. Again, he did not seek revenge.

I will tell you that there is so much more to Gabe's story, but this is not the place to tell it. We all have a past, and we must protect words that the enemy could use against God's people.

"God couldn't love me because I made a wrong choice," he explained to me in the car. "My brother-in-law was the one who was responsible for all the bad things that were done to me. When my sister left him to come and live with us, he took his two-year-old daughter and bashed her head to the floor in front of us."

At last Gabe couldn't take anymore. He put a gun to his brother-in-law's head. He threatened to kill him if he ever came close to the family again. He said that if anyone took his family or his Bible, that person would not be able to live.

As he was recounting his story for me, he pointed his finger straight at my head. He was getting jumpy, and I was growing alarmed.

Gabe explained that he called his priest then and said, "I made a bad decision and I am turning my life over to satan."

When he paused, I asked Gabe how serving satan was working for him and why he called me when I obviously have no use for satan?

"I am not sure. I saw your eyes today and the Bible. I recognized you, and I knew you would not hurt me. I wanted you to know how bad I am," he said.

Gabe seemed both repentant and hopeless. I started to cry, but I knew I had to stay strong in the Spirit. The enemy is no match for God's Spirit, yet I know he can influence my flesh. This was spiritual warfare like I had never experienced, and it was happening inside the tortured man next to me.

I was terrified, but I wasn't going to let Gabe see it. I had just found out he was worshipping satan, and now he was looking at me like I was his enemy. He unzipped his coat and threw it in my back seat. My fear grew.

"Okay, Lord," I prayed. "I am here and I know You sent me."

Gabe then said, "I am retarded, and I have done many things wrong. God could never love me."

"That is a lie!" I retorted. "Your sin is no greater than my sin. If you are retarded, you would not know it. It is a lie! You were made for God, not satan!"

"You don't know anything. I am evil and I have no respect for God," he said, pulling up shirt sleeves. "Look at my arms."

He had an upside-down cross tattooed on his shoulder and another cross carved on the inside of his forearm. The latter in particular was horrible looking. Gabe explained that he'd carved it with a knife after he had threatened to kill his brother-in-law. He said the four points were for his four years of seminary, and the center was for satan.

"So what?" I said. "I have scars you can't see. They are all the same, and Jesus still loves us."

I told him about the woman I'd met in Zimbabwe and how she had murdered babies to be used for witchcraft. Yet I saw Christ in her, just like I could see Christ in Gabe. I told him that Jesus had never left him and that satan is scared of him and what he knows in Christ.

"Satan does not want you to follow Jesus because he knows how powerful the Holy Spirit is," I added.

Gabe said that bad things had happened to him when he was trying to make good decisions and that meant God had left him.

"No! That is a lie. It was satan who did the bad things because he does not want you with the Lord."

Now Gabe unbuttoned his shirt to show me his chest. His skin was covered in horrifying scars, all rough and raw looking. I didn't ask why he had them or what happened, and he didn't offer to explain. *Do I run or stay, Lord?* I couldn't move, so I knew God wanted me to stay at Gabe's side. Though I was scared in my flesh, I was bold in my spirit.

Gabe reached into his pocket, and I knew he had a weapon. He pulled out a single bullet and rested it on my dashboard. He told me he had planned to quit his job that day and kill himself on the way home. I immediately grabbed the bullet and put it on top of my Bible.

"No, Gabe," I said. "We are not going to let the enemy win. Do you really think he will stop here? He will go after your mom, your dad and your sister. God is trusting you to stay here to protect them. Gabe, you have everything you need inside of you."

"I don't have anything but evil in me," he repeated. "I have lost everything."

Gabe reached again into his pocket, and I knew what was coming next. *If I die, God, I still know You sent me here.* He pulled out a gun, holding it for a moment.

"Gabe, you don't want to hurt anyone," I said firmly.

I knew God wanted me here on earth to love His people, so I claimed protection in the name of Jesus.

"Gabe, let me have the gun!" I insisted.

To my amazement, he quietly handed it to me. *This moment gave God's breath away.* I opened the car door and placed the gun on the ground outside.

"You cannot do that," he said. "They will use it to hurt someone."

I couldn't believe I was taking advice from a man who claimed to serve satan and had just handed me a gun, but I opened the door and carefully placed the weapon inside on the floor.

I continued telling Gabe how much God loves him when he reached into his pocket another time. Bold now, I shouted, "Gabe, enough!" He opened his hand to show me a fistful of bullets. He handed them to me; I put them on the floor with the gun.

I kept talked to Jessie, telling him he wasn't supposed to die and that God had sent me to tell him how much he was loved. Gabe told me he'd tried once before to end his life but the gun did not go off. He asked me to give him the gun back so he could show me what went wrong. I refused.

"Gabe," I pleaded. "If I was going to kill myself and God sent you to stop me, I hope you would love me enough not to give the gun to me."

If the truth be known, I was afraid that if I gave him the gun he would use it on me. I could see and feel when the enemy took Gabe; it was like two different people in one.

He settled down and grabbed my hand. He seemed to need the comfort of contact. In my hands I still had my Bible and the single bullet. I asked Gabe if I could read about love from First Corinthians.

"Yes," he said.

He did not want to let go of my hand. I put my reading glasses on, trying to joke that I was old and needed them to see.

"You are not old. You are the most beautiful woman I have ever seen."

I knew Gabe was going in a bad direction again. I could sense him testing me, pushing me to condemn him and kick him out of my car. Instead I placed his hand firmly on his own lap and said, "The only beauty you see in me is Christ—and don't you forget it."

He cowered at my words. I read to him from Galatians, about the Fruit of the Spirit and emphasized *"don't get weary in doing good."* I read him the entire chapter on love in First Corinthians. He didn't utter a word, but simply sat and wept.

The moment I finished reading, a knock came on my car window. It was a police officer, an angel, a gift from God! He opened my car door and saw the gun.

"Ma'am, what is going on here?" he asked.

I briefly explained, and he asked Gabe to step out of the car. Gabe admitted the gun was stolen, and the officer asked me to write a statement. As the officer escorted Gabe to the police car, he turned back to me. He held up his handcuffed arms and said with disgust, "See? This is what your God does to me."

"Don't you even talk about our God like that!" I told him. "You know perfectly well you opened yourself up to satan, and he is the one who comes to kill and destroy."

Gabe started to cry again, and then he disappeared into the back seat of the cruiser.

I asked the officer if I could speak to Gabe one more time. He advised against it, but I didn't back down. I went to Gabe and told him about Apostle Paul, how even in prison he was free. Gabe said he doubted that he would ever be free.

"You are free in Christ," I reminded him. "God sent me to tell you."

Before the officer drove away, I asked him why he had stopped and knocked on my window. He said, "I don't know. Nothing looked strange; I just stopped!"

I let him know that God sent him in response to my prayer, then thanked him for being obedient and listening. I told him that God had used him to help me end my appointment. We spoke for a moment about church and missions, and he said he'd like to go to Africa someday.

I was not wise to come to this appointment alone, yet in Christ we are never alone! He sends others to cover our shortcomings. I generally don't like to point out the shortcomings in others; rather, I want to be the person who covers them.

I left the parking lot and for a time suppressed the emotions and sensations of what had just happened. I needed to stop at Wal-Mart to buy some more things for my grandson and then go to church. In the store parking lot, I got out of my car only to immediately see one of the police officers. He told me I was lucky to get out unscathed and urged me to be more careful. He suggested that I stay away from the restaurant for a while and avoid future contact with Gabe. I thanked him and went on my way.

After I finished my errands, I reflected on my time with Gabe and began to cry. I had to pull off the road so I could safely weep. God had just worked through me in a mighty way, and I was overwhelmed by the experience.

I remembered that Gabe had asked me to call his girlfriend, Samantha, and talk with her. I was not at all sure I wanted her to have my phone number, but true to my word I called her. Her voice and attitude were sweet, and we prayed together. She told me that Gabe had indeed gone to seminary, and she confirmed that he had been worshipping satan. I prayed with her on the phone and later found out she also was worshiping satan.

As I hung up the phone with Samantha, a call came in. The woman told me she was calling from a hospital, where Gabe had been taken. Gabe had told her she needed to talk with me and that I would pick him up because I was the only one he would trust. She added that Gabe had talked about me the entire length of his hospital visit.

I asked the woman if I could speak with Gabe and explain why I couldn't pick him up. I told him what the police officer said, and he seemed okay with my answer.

He called again later that night, at 10:39 p.m., to let me know he was home and not to worry. He said he would be back at work the next day.

By then I was ready to sleep, to check out for a few hours and not think any more. I slept until my alarm went off hours later.

As I woke up, I remembered dreaming about fire and how it couldn't burn me or even get near me. Now, as I reflect on God's heart, even with all of the horrible things I had heard from Gabe, one thought overpowered all. Gabe did not have a Bible, and I knew I had to get him one immediately. My next thought was straight from God: *Let yesterday be yesterday and today be today.*

Today, I would get him a Bible. I was thankful God had more for Gabe.

On Sundays, Brian and I are committed to serving at an inner-city church. That morning I felt strangely like a swan — so peaceful and calm on the surface, but underneath I was anxiously paddling like a duck. I had only until 3:00 p.m. — the end of Gabe's shift — to get a Bible. It had to be today; timing is important to God.

With the original disciples, Jesus communicated differently with each according to their needs. Most days He gives me puzzle pieces so I can understand His purpose for me. He never rushes me or makes me feel like I cannot understand. Sometimes I don't even know what I'm *not* getting until the last piece falls into place. This day, the Lord gave me what I thought was the whole puzzle. I was sure of what I hoped for and certain of what God would deliver.

After church I dropped off Brian at home and prayed all the way to the bookstore. As I looked through the selection of

Bibles, I felt I was the only person on Earth—just God and me. He makes each one of us feel so valuable if we let Him!

God put it on my heart to give Gabe a *God Calling* devotional, too. I could not stop thinking about how Gabe's life was about to change. I pictured myself going to his church one day and hearing him preach.

I pulled into the restaurant parking lot right at 3:00 p.m. as several workers were locking the doors. I handed the Bible to one lady, who said she would take it to Gabe.

He called about an hour later to say "thank you" over and over. I told him I would be eagerly waiting to visit his church and hear him preach. I knew he needed something to have faith in. Most of all, he needs love and forgiveness.

But God is guiding me to draw back just now. Gabe called again a few evenings later, and I did not pick up his call. I have to be still and know that God will do the rest.

A friend told me not to worry about Gabe. Another of God's people will come to water the seeds that God has planted. I believe!

Chapter 15

Does God Say Thank You?

M y "thank you" came late one night when my phone rang. It was Gabe, the young man who had professed to worship satan and had intended to take his own life. In my flesh I had two choices: to answer or not to answer. In my spirit, I had only one choice.

Lord, if this is you, I will know you by your voice.

I answered the call and instantly recognized something different in Jessie. I didn't have to ask questions or even talk, because Gabe was obviously filled with God's love.

"Bobbie, I owe you my life," he said. "My mother gave me minutes on my phone so I could call you. She has been crying and wants to thank you."

In the background, Jessie spoke with her in Spanish. I could not understand her words, but I understood her message. (I am a mother and a daughter, too!)

Gabe told me the story of his day on September 6, 2009. We were together that day, yet our stories were different. I wish I could have recorded his phone call; it was one of the sweetest things I could have experienced. I wept quietly with my hands to the Lord as he talked. I didn't ask for confirmation from God; I was at perfect peace knowing I went for God, yet He wanted me to know my work had not been in vain.

I want to share Gabe's words with you now:

"Thank you, Bobbie. I owe you my life. I started my day not wanting to live. I said to myself, *There is no reason to live*. I did not steal the gun; I bought it because I have never stolen anything in my life. When I got to work, I was thinking as I looked at everyone that today would be the last time I would see them. Then I looked up and saw you. There is something about your eyes. I could see Jesus, and then I saw your Bible. When you told me that Christ was in my heart and not to worry that I had not gone to church in four years, I knew you were real. When you gave me your phone number, I was not planning on calling. I went to the back and threw your and your husband's cards in the trash.

"Later in the day, I could not get you off my mind. I told myself you were not real and that you would not talk with me if I called you. Then I went to the trash and tried to find your cards. I could not find them and got in trouble for wasting time at work. When I was cleaning out my pockets during my break, your card was in my pocket. I held it and could not believe it. I knew I threw both of the cards away! That is when I called you.

"As I dialed, I thought, *She will not answer*. When you did, I thought, *She will not be able to meet me today*. When you said 'yes,' I hung up the phone and thought, *She will not come*. I was happy and then I thought I would scare you and tell you how bad I am. You would tell me to get out of your car and then I would go to the trees."

Gabe told me that the trees were where he planned to go to kill himself. He then recapped every moment we spent together in the car.

"First I was going to tell you all of the stories, and when that didn't work I thought, *I will tell her I worship Satan and she will tell me to get out!* You just looked at me with your eyes. I thought, *I know, the gun will do it*. When that didn't work, I thought, *I will scare her by getting close to her*. But you did not move. You started to read me the Bible. Right before the police came, I thought about Job and how God let satan take everything but his life. I knew at that moment God sent you for me. That is when the police knocked on your window."

As I listened to Gabe, I realized why God gave me courage that day. Gabe asked me if God was upset with him for wanting to kill himself. "No," I said. "He *loves* you."

I told Jessie that he did not have time to grow roots and that we can all have head knowledge of the Bible, but that is not good enough. Like when he took the Bible from church to his home, the peace did not come with it. God built his church on revelation—the Holy Spirit working inside of us. That is why we must learn from the Word and then live God's Word through the Holy Spirit. I told him I am still learning, and that he cannot even trust me with God's direction for his life.

"I am just a person trying to help God love His people, and you do not owe me your life," I said. "I did not die for you, Gabe. Jesus died for you!"

I continued, "You saw the Holy Spirit work on Saturday. I came to see you because God loves you so much that He sent me to tell you. Do you realize I am thankful for your life? Please understand that my life was changed that day also. I love Jesus with all of my heart and I got to see His love for you. The way He loves others teaches me more than Him loving me. Even though you tried to scare me—and believe me, I was scared in my flesh—my spirit could only see your goodness. My spirit did not see your scars and your inner wounds. Think for a minute what I experienced that day. The teaching here is deeper than our human minds can grasp. When I am in His Spirit, I have the heart of God! He showed me how much He loved you; He showed me again that He does not measure sin. He measures faith, Gabe. I came in faith and you came in faith! He never left you, Gabe…. He has been with you the whole time."

Gabe spoke again. "Bobbie, I told my mom that I would not let you down. I am going to be a pastor." *This moment gave God's breath away.*

He then told me stories from when he lived in California, beautiful stories about what he did in the church and who he prayed for. He even healed several people who were near death. His friends told him he'd be rich if he charged money for the healings. He told them, "I am rich in God's love."

Of course there is more to this story — some treasures God wants me to keep quietly in my heart. I'm not sure if this day was for Gabe or for me. Each day, Jesus shows me who He really is and how valuable His children are to Him. I love how He loves; it's not something to be grasped in our flesh. In faith I know He will continue to use His Spirit in me to bring hope, faith and love. The greatest of these is love. I am thankful because love is the one easiest for me. (I'm still working on the hope and faith.) Meanwhile I am loving this seed time, which gives God time to make all things possible.

Chapter 16

Self-Evaluation Needed

This morning my God Appointment was with myself! It really was everything I never knew I needed (the keyword is "needed"). Why is it we can go through life loving, learning and teaching yet never seeing our own weaknesses?

This morning God gently let me know I was not leaving room for ALL of His people. I even tried to fight Him a little and defend myself. He reminded me that I don't need to defend myself *or* Him. When I defend myself, I assume I am right and someone else thinks I am wrong.

God then went one step further in my correction. In love He let me know I was not wrong, I was weary. Galatians 6:9 says, *"Let us not become weary in doing good, for at the proper time we will reap a harvest if we do not give up."* I am thankful that God reads our hearts and does not give much time to our flesh.

The last several days I've been frantically searching for a Hispanic church for my friend, Gabe. I wanted to help him find a congregation where he belonged and could worship on Saturday nights. My heart was in the right place, yet my mind was limited to what I know in this world. Through experience I've learned that when I limit myself to only my thoughts, I also limit God's people. When I live by His Spirit, I empower God's people.

It has been several weeks since Gabe tried to take his life. In our growing relationship, we have experienced some good days and bad days. The enemy does not give up, and that is fine. He is no match for the Holy Spirit, yet he can maneuver our minds.

In my search for a church, I called all of my friends to see if they knew of a Hispanic church on Saturday night. I thought, *Come on, people, how hard can it be to find a church for this guy?* I was already starting to point a finger!

At the beginning of the week, I promised Gabe we would go to church together that Saturday. But to Gabe the church represented many broken promises, so he wasn't excited about going. He had fallen into a mindset of blaming the church for many of the awful experiences that happened while he was in seminary.

"Bobbie, I don't want to go, but I will go for you," he said.

That was good enough for me, because I had an agenda, right? By Saturday morning, I still hadn't turned up a church. Gabe called and asked what time we would pick him up. I told him we were on and moved ahead in faith. Yet I was growing increasingly *unpeaceful* with this process. I was running late for my grandson Andreas' basketball game, which added to my unease.

During the game, I badgered my daughter Billie about finding a church for Gabe. In between plays I encouraged her to use her phone to search. Finally she said, "Why don't you take him to an English-speaking church? He speaks English, right?"

Um…that was a thought, but I wanted him to be around people like him. In my heart I wanted a support system for Gabe, and I was thinking with what I know in my mind — which always limits me. Remember, the enemy can only work with what we know. The Spirit is filled with what God knows. I realized this once again and smiled. Through my daughter, He spoke to me. She said, "Mom, take him to our church. They are doing a series on resetting your life."

I picked Gabe up at 4:00 p.m. When he walked out dressed in a suit I almost cried. It was like seeing your child all dressed up for his first day of school. His formal dress represented respect for God. He had been worshipping satan for the last four years and had many scars to prove it. Today he wanted me to see him in a new way.

I could tell he was a little nervous — and truthfully so was I. I wanted this to be a good experience, and I was worried he wouldn't like this church because it was different for him. I reminded myself Jesus built his church on the revelation Peter had about who Jesus was — not on Peter the man or a specific building. Here I'd been so concerned about the church building, the pastor speaking, the language, the type of people, the music and so on that I didn't leave anything up to God.

When we arrived at church, I was feeling a little embarrassed. I'd just picked him up at a trailer park and took him to what looks like the Taj Mahal in comparison. *Here I go, judging a book by its cover again. I have so much mercy for God's people, and yet I am not so merciful on the church. How can that be?*

But the church is nothing more than God's people. We walked in, and everyone greeted us with so much love. The moment I saw God's people, I forgot about how big the building was.

As we walked into the sanctuary I thought, *He is not going to like this music.* I was so preoccupied I could hardly worship. Guess what? He did not like the music.

When it was time for the message, I was listening only to think about what was Gabe thinking. My memory of this moment takes me back to a passage from my *God Calling* devotional: *"It is like a weary man on a hot and dusty road bearing a heavy load, when all plans have been made for its carriage. The road, scenery, flowers, beauty around all have been lost."* I am reminded each day that the Word of God is living and it sets me free.

From *God Calling*, published by Barbour Publishing, Inc. Used by permission.

I began listening to the message in earnest and forgot that Gabe was even with me. The pastor was teaching us about the prodigal son. Today the message had new meaning. I'd spent the week talking with Gabe about the people who wouldn't let him out of the box he had put himself in.

My father used to say, "Bobbie, we gave you your name, but you will put meaning behind that name." Gabe had years of meaning behind his name. The pastor talked about how the Pharisees were judgmental; it seemed like the perfect message for Gabe. It was living, it was God. It was everything I know, and yet in my mind I still doubted.

As the service ended and we left the auditorium, Gabe talked and talked. "This is a message straight from God," he said. "I know He is calling me. This is the church I was supposed to come to today."

The gift didn't stop there. I noticed communion was being served in the chapel. I sat down but kept my eyes open. I watched Gabe go up and receive communion. He knelt in the seat in front of me, holding his bread and cup near his heart. *This moment gave God's breath away.*

Is this how God feels when He sees us turn our lives over to Him each day? God loves us so much, and I want Him to have the pleasure I felt in the chapel as I watched Gabe experience His wonders.

When Gabe got in the car, I said, "I was so afraid you wouldn't like the music."

"I didn't like the music," he said. "But it was the message I came for — not the music."

Heaven on Earth is everywhere. I know that Heaven is in me. Jesus left it for me and you. We don't have to worry about a church building or denomination or music, because He will find us wherever and whenever we are. We can't find a perfect church because it is made of people — and people are made of body, soul/mind and spirit. As we focus on bringing heaven to earth the Holy Spirit will take more people to heaven.

When I point a finger, I hope I will realize right away that three fingers are pointing back at me. Together, we can pull in the pointing finger to join the others and leave the thumb up towards to God. He will take our burdens, and we will be left not only to follow Him but to imitate Him, too.

Chapter 17

The Second Love

I cannot imagine my life without God Appointments. I pray daily for God to bring people that need to hear His words, and yet somehow I'm always amazed when He chooses to give His *breath* away through me. Each time is like the first time. I believe that was God's intention when He designed our relationship with Him ("First Love") and when He designed our relationship with our spouse ("Second Love").

I woke up one recent day thinking, *Maybe I won't pray today for God Appointments.* I was trying to finish this book, and each day God would give me one more journal, or chapter, to add. If I could just take a couple of days off, I could complete the book. So I held back my prayer for about an hour and then said, "Lord, I cannot do it."

Now, I don't remember the last time I didn't pray for an appointment with God. So I prayed anyway! In faith I knew that God would end this book in His time and until then, I would just keep praying and writing.

At work, I passed my friend Russ. We exchanged the normal hellos, and for some reason I said, "I would like to hear about your girls." Russ has two beautiful young daughters, Rachel and Jessica. I've been friends with the family since the girls were little.

After talking, Russ and I jumped back into a busy pace and proceeded to get some work done. As I was checking my e-mails in my office, I heard the sweetest voice from the doorway: "Hello, Bobbie!" It was Russ's daughter Jessica.

Unknown to me, she'd been waiting outside in the car. Russ had gone out to tell her I'd like to see her. Immediately I knew this was a God Appointment. I did not know why or what, I just knew I was available.

I gave Jessica a great big hug and invited her and her dad to sit down. I shared news about my family, our new grandbaby, Corbin, and the great news about our grandson, Keontaye, and his new family.

Our mission pastor always asks young people what they are going to do with their lives, and then he waits for the treasure to unfold. This is such a beautiful question, because every life is worth knowing about. I asked this question of Jessica, and she eagerly told me about her college plans. She mentioned how valuable her friends were to her.

The next part of our conversation revealed the reason God called this meeting.

"Bobbie, Jessica has a boyfriend," Russ said.

Of course, this news made me giggle and smile. Even at my age, I continue to marvel at the miracle of true love.

"I love that," I said. "Tell me about him."

Jessica said they'd been friends all through school. This struck me for two reasons: one, because they'd been friends; and two, their friendship had lasted a period of time.

I've discovered that when relationships happen in the God-intended order, we are able to see the other person as he or she is without us—not as the person who pleases us for the moment. In every relationship, there are times we are not pleased. When a relationship is built on the foundation of friendship, we can see past our own needs and into the heart of the other person. This insight helps us make better choices when we select our Second Love.

Jessica had no way of knowing that God had placed this on my heart. She could not have known that I didn't feel worthy to teach her or anyone else about pure love. She could not have known that God was calling me to write a book called *The Second Love*. She could not have known I was not moving ahead with the book because, well, as you know I am far from pure.

I started to share with Jessica all the things God had recently put on my heart about love. I told her about a book I was reading, *And the Bride Wore White* by Dannah Gresh. If you asked me why I was reading a book on sexual purity, I would tell you, "I don't know other than that God wants me to." Russ mentioned that he'd heard Dannah on the radio and had told his wife, Lori, that he'd love the girls to read that book.

I'd only read the first chapter, and I realized then that God intended for Jessica to have my copy. Once again, God put me in a position to give because I have, not because I want.

The words that flowed from my mouth were healing and beautiful. Most of all, they were a revelation to me about God's intentions for our First Love to be with God Himself and the Second Love to be with our partner in life. With this appointment, God confirmed that He is willing to write another book through me.

Jessica looked like a little girl ready to hear a bedtime story. Her eyes were bright and full of hope. She wanted to know more about the Second Love, and I wanted to know more about God's intentions.

I'd already realized how amazing our relationship can be with Christ through the Holy Spirit; it is much more than I knew even about the First Love. I couldn't help but think there was more to the Second Love that I had not experienced. Because God had revealed to me all He had about the First Love through *God Appointments*, in faith I believe He will reveal His intentions for the Second Love. I haven't known many people who have accepted what I believe God **intended** for the First Love or Second Love here on earth.

One day in prayer I asked God, "Why did you make me?"

Not "Bobbie" specifically, but "woman." This question led to more thoughts, more prayers and more reading. The answer is in the Bible, but God knew I needed a little help. Asking this question led me to the appointment in my office with Jessica.

I told her I was proud of her and emphasized the importance of friendship in having a Second Love with her eventual husband. Their relationship with each other would imitate their individual relationships with the First Love (God). I talked to her about the garden with Adam and Eve, and how Adam had everything he could ever want or dream of—yet he was missing something still. I shared how the first challenge was not sin, but loneliness. I told her my favorite part is how God didn't get jealous and say, "Adam, you are so spoiled! All you need is me!" Instead, God observed Adam and determined that his creation needed a Second Love. Well, you know what happens next. God made Eve out of Adam's rib and gave us His order.

"Follow my example, as I follow the example of Christ. I praise you for remembering me in everything and for holding to the teachings just as I passed them on to you. Now I want you to realize that the head of every man is Christ, and the head of the woman is man, and the head of Christ is God. —1 Corinthians 11:1-3

I wanted Jessica to know how much a man can desire and love a woman when he trusts who she is and why she comes. Just like the relationship between God and Jesus, we too can experience that type of spiritual love with the Second Love. I believe that God's intention for the Second Love is a man, who is after a woman, who was made for a man, who is after God's heart.

I described how God gave Adam armor against the enemy and how Adam knew to resist the devil's tricks. Have you ever wondered why the enemy didn't go after Adam before

Eve was created? It seems it would've been easier to trick one person rather than two.

As I spoke with Jessica, I realized Adam had the armor from God to defend himself from the enemy—and Satan knew he was no match for Adam. Eve herself didn't need armor because she was to be under the protection and authority of Adam. And Adam would have protected her at all cost.

I also believe Adam's armor had a little hole for Eve, his Second Love. He loved her so much and wanted to please her. God instilled this desire in Adam's heart because He knew Eve could respect her husband, complement him and give him strength. This very love led Adam to please Eve even against the one he loved most, His Father. Adam's eventual mistake changed many things drastically—but it did not change the love God and Adam had for each other.

With Jessica's eager attention, I continued—explaining that women today can get jealous of men's time and attention. We know how much Adam loved God; in the garden he spent his days walking with and worshiping God. Eve also loved God and would not intentionally hurt Him or Adam.

No doubt the enemy watched these relationships grow. He knew what buttons to push to make Eve think she could get more love and attention—like Adam gave to God—if she possessed God's full knowledge. This is the picture God has put on my heart to help me understand the Second Love.

I explained to Jessica the lengths her Second Love (her husband) would undoubtedly go to please her. And not just to ensure her pleasure but to fulfill his God-given desire and design. He would want to please her in many ways, like Adam wanted to please Eve. But their relationship would have to remain in God's order. Just like Eve, we don't always operate in this order—but those who know Christ always get another chance to please God.

I shared that a woman was made to create an environment where a man could become who God intended him to be. In this special design, we get all the love, attention, time and authentic joy we could hope for.

As my conversation with Jessica came to an end, she hugged me twice and said, "Thank you so much." *This moment gave God's breath away.*

I love how young people can see what can be. My prayer is that somehow I can help people find and embrace God's intention for their First Love and Second Love.

A special note to anyone who is not young or has already blown every order known to mankind: I join you in the ranks. I just know what I have experienced with the First Love, and through Christ all things are possible. I'm not saying I am an expert (or even good) at this Second Love thing. I have so much yet to learn. But if it can be anything like the First Love, I want it — here on Earth and in Heaven.

Chapter 18

Decision Points

Mother Teresa said it best: "Small things done in great love can change the world."

Many of these God Appointments seem big here on earth. I must say now that the small ones give me the courage to experience the big ones. If God doesn't measure sin, surely He doesn't measure our appointments. Rather, He delights in our faith.

Every God Appointment is valuable to Him, and I know from experience that each appointment begins with a decision point. Each decision point involves a yes, no, or maybe — and sometimes all three at the same time.

I was telling a friend the other day how my life is funny. By now you'd think I would just accept each and every God Appointment. Yet I decide or change my mind in two seconds or sometimes two weeks or more. But what's important is not how long we take to make the decision, but that we decide to accept the God Appointments set for us.

Only after my first mission trip did I begin to journal my experiences, and even then I recorded only what really moved me. I was more comfortable with my everyday God Appointments and didn't think to journal them. I hadn't yet learned about measurement and the value of what God sees.

Now I would like to share some of the "small" Decision Points that have occurred as I accepted God Appointments. I cannot judge how big or small they are to God or to the people He sends me. My job is to be willing when He puts the appointment on my heart.

Please understand there is nothing special about *me*. And maybe that's why I have so many appointments. Regardless of intelligence, education or ability here on earth, the common thread among those who have God Appointments is a willingness to pray, ask, listen, learn and accept. I hope you do, too, because *each moment will give God's breath away!*

Give What?

One time the Lord told me to give my Bible away. Mind you, it was not just any Bible. It was the one I'd carried through the toughest season of my life. It looked like it had been through a war and was marked throughout with my personal notes.

At a fitness class I attended, I became friends with the instructor, Derek. While talking one day, he shared some of the struggles he'd been through. Several weeks later, the Lord put it on my heart to give Derek my Bible.

My first response? *No, not my Bible, Lord!*

I'd already told my daughter Robbie Sue she could have it when I died. She reminded me often that she wanted my Bible one day. So for days I thought of reasons why Derek did not need my Bible. *What's the big deal?* I thought. *I could buy him a Bible.*

But no matter how I tried to rationalize it, I could not find peace. This was a battle waging between my mind and spirit—and I knew what I had to do.

Even in my obedience, I wanted to do things my own way. And the amazing thing is, that decision was okay with God. He gave me a couple of days to copy my notes to another Bible.

Don't be impressed with my decision. When I gave my Bible to Derek, I said that God wanted me to give him my

Bible, but I didn't want to. He said, "Bobbie, that's okay. You don't have to give it to me."

I explained that I needed to do this for the Lord and that God must have a big plan for Derek's life. Now I know the Lord did this for me. As I walked away, God gave me the most amazing peace. And I knew I'd need that peace as I explained the situation to my daughter.

Turns out I had a hair appointment with Robbie Sue that same day. I was scared to sit down in her chair at the salon. Through prayer, I found the words to tell her.

Robbie and my other daughter, Billie, are hair stylists. At the time, they worked in the same shop and their chairs were next to each other. When I told them what I had done, both girls looked at me like I'd given away my firstborn child. Robbie told me that one of her recent clients had talked about how she was saving her Bible for her son.

Wow. For a minute, I felt like a big loser.

Almost instantly, He renewed my mind and the words flowed boldly with a touch of love.

"Girls, the very reason I am able to love you like I do is because of the love I have for the Lord," I said. "No one wanted you to have my Bible more than me—and that would have been fine. But the Lord trumped it. How can I walk in His love and not give for Him in faith?"

I never want my daughters to put me first before the Lord. And I guess I had to teach them that with my behavior.

The most beautiful thing happened several months later. Derek told me he would make sure my daughter got my Bible someday. My daughters are two of the most amazing woman today because they know who they are in Christ!

Shoeshine, Anyone?

I was walking through an airport and saw a gentleman at the shoeshine stand. I could see pain on his face.

The thought came that I should stop and get my boots shined. But I kept walking and covered this thought with some of my own. *I don't have time. I have to get my luggage. My boots don't need to be polished. I am almost out of security. I would have to walk all the way back.*

These were all great excuses. Yet not one of them came with any peace. I stopped in my tracks...and turned around, smiling all the while. I love God so much and after these little squabbles I find Him even more loving.

I arrived at the shoeshine stand and the chair was open. The gentleman was very quiet and he didn't want to talk. Turns out he couldn't speak English, but he could understand it.

The other shoe-shiner at the stand started to talk with me. Amazingly, he was from Zimbabwe. He talked about his son and how he sends money to keep him in school. We talked about God and the Holy Spirit. I shared how God's Spirit can help him find his way. The other gentleman listened to every word as he shined my boots and smiled continuously. By the time my shoes were polished and shiny, the three of us prayed together.

I don't always know why these encounters happen, and that is fine. I am just a moment in time for God. I want to give because I have, not because I want.

Breaks or Brakes?

It was lunch break and I was on my way to get Chinese food. I had a big project at work and I didn't have much time to spare. In the parking lot, a young woman looking tired and weary was sitting on the curb. Her arm was in a cast and she was staring up at the sky. I drove by, but her face would not fade from my memory.

Back up!

That's how it always starts — with a thought — and most of the time it's a thought I don't want to act on. This time I thought, *I can't back up. There are cars behind me.* But I looked in the rearview mirror and saw no cars. Sighing, I hit the brakes, put the car in reverse and wondered just how nutty I was about to appear.

My car went backward, I rolled my window down, and I said, "Are you okay?" And then, "The Lord just told me to back up and check on you."

She started to cry. Through the tears she told me she was fine, but was frustrated with her life just then. Then she told me a car was waiting behind me. I heard a beeping horn and waved the car around.

Then I told the woman she was important to God, and He sent me to tell her how much He loves her. I told her to pray and give her burdens to Him so she could focus on healing.

She smiled and said, "Thank you so much. I know God sent you!"

As I drove away, I felt the most amazing peace. With each appointment, no matter how big or small, comes a joy from God loving others through us. It's just one of the gifts he gives when we say "yes" to His appointments.

Better Late Than Never

My next appointment stands out because the decision point came immediately. I was at a red light when a huge truck rammed into the back of my car. The impact was so loud I thought my car had exploded. I looked up to see the truck in my rear-view mirror.

My first thought was that I was going to be late for my meeting.

The other driver, a young man, looked like a large burly farm boy. With the sweetest tone he asked if I was hurt. I told him I was fine but that I was going to be late for a meeting. He apologized, saying he would call the police, and walked away.

The next thought that popped into my mind: *opportunity*. I instantly knew what God meant. I was out of my car in the next second, asking the driver if he was okay. He said he was and pointed to his truck, which didn't have a scratch.

"I don't mean your truck," I said. "I want to know if *you* are okay."

He wasn't hurt, he said, just overwhelmed with life. I told him I understood, that I felt the same way. I explained that the meeting I was going to was really important, but that I was thankful he'd hit me and I was glad to meet him.

I continued, telling him I sometimes had to be reminded that God's people are so important to Him. I told him I believed this was a God Appointment, and that I was excited for his life. I said that he must be in the middle of something really big for God to bring us together like this.

We laughed and talked briefly about how amazing God is. There we were, in the middle of a busy intersection, and we didn't even notice the traffic and the vehicles lining up behind us.

The police hadn't arrived yet, and now I know why. God gave us the time we needed. I asked the driver if I could pray for his life. He smiled, looked around and said, "Right now?"

"Yeah...why not?"

What a sweet moment. He shut his eyes and bowed his head. I didn't hear a sound. We were as alone as if we were standing in the middle of a faraway field.

After the prayer, we looked up to see a police officer standing next to us with his head down. The officer asked if we knew each other. I said, "Yes, sir. He just crashed into the back of my car — and now we're friends."

The officer looked at us like we were crazy. But it's so worth it to be crazy in love with God. He is faithful when we show up!

The Messenger

Her name is Patricia. I met her while waiting in line to check my grandkids into the childcare room for my Wednesday night Bible study. When she said "hello," I could hear that she was from somewhere other than Indiana.

We started to talk and I learned she was from Zimbabwe. I told her about Horizon International and how the organization worked with AIDS orphans in that area.

When I met Patricia, I hadn't been to Zimbabwe yet. In fact, I hadn't even thought of going there. I always went to South Africa to visit my sponsored children. We exchanged telephone numbers, but I didn't think I'd hear from her again.

Several weeks later, she called and asked if we could meet. She said she wasn't sure why she wanted to share her life with me, but felt that God brought me to her.

When we got together, Patricia told a story that made my heart ache. After her husband was killed in Zimbabwe, she moved to the United States, leaving her four-year-old daughter, Sikhumbuzo, behind. When Patricia arrived in the states, she learned there was no way to get her daughter out of Zimbabwe. And so she had not seen Sikhumbuzo in ten long years.

After our appointment, I thanked the Lord for trusting me with the details of Patricia's life. I reminded Him that I was available; I thanked Him for giving me a new friend. Little did I know, God had plans for me to be a messenger.

Months later, I got a call from our missions pastor, Doug, who said his wife Sandy was preparing to help lead a women's conference in Zimbabwe. He asked me to go along and share. I told him I'd go if he wanted me to, but I'd already made plans to visit South Africa. (Learn more in the "Zimbabwe and Eyes to See" chapter.)

I knew I was being disobedient, but I did not want to go to Zimbabwe. My thoughts bounced around wildly, trying to understand and justify why I didn't want to go. I couldn't find peace anywhere, yet I was sure I *did not want to go*. Still, I knew what I had to do.

I called Doug and told him I would go even though I did not want to. He was surprised by my less-than-bubbly attitude. With a laugh he said, "Maybe you should pray a little more."

When I told Patricia I was going to Zimbabwe, she cried. I was so ashamed, because deep down I still didn't want to go.

The day before I left, Patricia met me in a parking lot and gave me several gifts to take to her daughter. She put her hands on my face and said, "Please kiss my daughter for me." She sobbed as she held my hands in hers. "Bobbie, your hands are going to touch my daughter. Thank you, Bobbie. Thank you, Bobbie!"

Wow.

I pulled away with my arms full of Patricia's gifts, photos and a special item she'd made, and I prayed. *Dear God, please forgive me for not wanting to go.*

God confirmed, "I know you do not want to go. I know you are going for me." Again, He allowed me to think I was going for Him. I am learning!

My journal about the Zimbabwe trip reveals why I had to go—and why I needed new eyes to see. I discovered that the enemy absolutely did not want me to go to Zimbabwe. The revelation God gave me was so big that He had to put me in an environment where my heart was prepared to receive it. This spiritual warfare explains my reluctance and fear. My feelings of reluctance were not from God, and I needed extra time to reach my Decision Point.

Within God's mission I can help one child at a time. I've learned through experience that orphans come in all different packages and that you don't have to give birth to have a child. Most of all, I know now that you don't have to have a child to be a messenger!

In Zimbabwe I got to hold Patricia's daughter, Sikhumbuzo, in my arms. I felt eleven years of her mother's love rush through my body. I don't have words to tell you what happened to me as I embraced her. To be a mother is one thing. To intercede for a mother who has not held her child for eleven years cannot be discerned by our flesh. The only thing I will hold higher is when I get to see Patricia holding Sikhumbuzo in her own arms. I believe in faith that Patricia will see her daughter again.

Holding Sikhumbuzo brought heaven to earth.

Forgive and Forget?

Yes, we should forgive all things. However, *not* forgetting can be a gentle reminder that sometimes we need to protect God's people from ourselves.

Most of the chapters in this book have been about the God Appointments I was able to receive. I thought I was done with this book when God recalled an appointment that happened many years ago. It was very painful; I buried it deep in my past.

Know that I have missed many God Appointments over the years. I say that in faith because I don't know what I don't know. It's easier that way. When God trusts us with one of His people and we hurt that individual—even when we don't mean to—the feeling is far worse than not getting the appointment at all.

When I think this, I remember what a dear friend always says: "Do *something* even if it is wrong."

The enemy would like me to focus on what I do wrong. God teaches me to focus on what He can do right through me. And God can use all things to His Glory. While I am forgiven, some experiences He does not want me to forget. God shows me that I am not the main event. He can carry out His will with or without me.

Brian and I were attending a weekend motivational conference with many of our friends. A young woman named Lilly was there, too. She had been hanging out with our networking group for about a year, and I knew God had brought her to me.

Lilly was inhibited in many ways, both in appearance and within. She was intelligent, yet she didn't believe in the Lord. I took it upon myself to love and spend time with her. She challenged me often, usually in front of our friends.

People in our group questioned what I saw in her. They said she would never come to know the Lord. But I knew my goal was not to **save** her; only God could save her. I just wanted to love her in the hope she would come to love the same Father I love and who loves us.

The weekend was great! I was all filled and ready for the Sunday morning church service. For most of the conference, seats were assigned, and the other members of the group and I were not able to sit together. But the Sunday service offered open seating. Even after just a few hours of sleep, I was motivated to get up early to **save** seats.

I said goodbye to Lilly Saturday night. She had never come to the church service at any previous conferences we'd attended together. In passing I teasingly said, "I'll miss you at church."

She smiled and replied, "I won't miss you."

The church service was packed. Fortunately I'd saved the exact number of seats for the people who'd planned to attend. One by one, our friends showed up to claim their spot.

As the service began and the music played, I felt a tap on my shoulder. There stood Lilly, asking me if I'd saved a seat for her.

"Oh, Lilly," I blurted. "They're all taken. I did not know you were coming, otherwise I would have **saved** you one." I gave her a hug and figured she would simply grab a single seat in the back of the room. I'm ashamed to say that several songs had been played before I heard God's voice: "You had a seat to give. You had your seat."

I jumped up and searched the auditorium for Lilly. She was nowhere.

As I began to cry, I went to the hotel lobby to find out if she'd checked out of her room. Still she was nowhere to be found.

I missed the entire church service and was utterly broken-hearted. In less than a second, I had done something very wrong. My relationship with Lilly had been a year of tough love. She was not easy on me, and even though I understand that hurt people *hurt people*, many times I was glad she did not show up for gatherings.

Now I realize that Lilly was pushing me away because she assumed someday I'd leave her anyway. Yet I also know that no matter what we do, God never leaves us. I left Lilly that day in the church service — but God did not leave me and He hasn't left Lilly.

I haven't seen Lilly again, but I trust today that He found someone to show her that He does not leave His people. I wish it had been me. I believe God wanted me to write about this particular God Appointment so we can protect His people. My prayer is that God used — or uses — someone with the right Decision Point to bring Lilly to Jesus. *I hope it's you!*

Childlike Faith Welcomed

This God Appointment occurred while I was writing what I thought to be the final chapter of this book. As you know, this book is not my own. The very fact that I am writing a book is a bigger miracle than these pages.

I'd had a tough day at work and was feeling down about what I had to offer. I questioned why anyone would want to read about God Appointments. I doubted why God had chosen me.

Seeking solitude, I went to my favorite bookstore to read over my manuscript drafts in peace. Sitting there by myself,

I thought how alone I felt. I doubted that I could be a good example to anyone with my brain full of negative thoughts.

At that very moment, God brought me three angels. It was Rachel, one of the students from our South Africa trip, with her two friends.

Oh dear, I am not going to be alone after all, I thought.

Then God took over for me. The girls and I talked about their evening and some of their challenges. The conversation helped me understand why we always need something bigger than ourselves.

Rachel's mom, my friend Theresa, winked at me as she walked around a corner and saw the girls sitting at my feet. As I love to do, I shared with the girls how God loves them and how He wants to love other young people through them. They asked me if that was what my book was about. I described the book, explained to them about God Appointments and told them we can learn to hear God's voice by understanding how we were made and the gifts we are given to communicate with the Lord.

I emphasized that they already have everything they need in Christ. They just need to understand what they have. The three grew excited through our conversation, saying they wanted to read the book and be available for God Appointments.

I knew they'd already started on that path—because today *I* was their God Appointment. God knew I needed His love and encouragement, and He chose three young girls who were willing. And, I should note, one mother who chose to listen to God's voice. This appointment gave me my belief back.

Later, Rachel's mom revealed that she'd seen my car at the bookstore, and God put it on her heart to send the girls in to find me. God allowed me to experience Heaven on Earth—not because I was listening to Him, but because others were listening to Him.

Seed Time

One of my dear friends always says, "You can count the seeds in an apple, but you cannot count the apples in a seed."

I'd just gotten off the phone with my friend, Gabe. In the chapter "God or Gun?," I described my appointment with this important young man, who had been worshiping satan and had decided to kill himself. He was calling this day to tell me his friend Samantha had been hit by a car and killed. The first day I spoke with Gabe, I had talked to her on the phone and prayed with her.

Gabe told me Samantha had accepted Jesus as her Savior the day *before* her accident, which gave me great comfort. She had moved to California in the months just after Gabe found the Lord again. She had been uncomfortable with his renewed love for Jesus and acted out by trying to hurt him and tempt him to return to his old habits. Yet Gabe stood firm and encouraged her to turn from satan and toward Jesus. I'm so proud and thankful that he never gave up on Samantha's life.

One day he was reading the Bible to her, and she noticed the *God Calling* devotional book I'd given him. "You need to give this to me," she said.

She would tease him and say she was going to steal it. Gabe would laugh and say, "You can't have it because Bobbie gave it to me."

When Samantha moved away to California, she took the book without Gabe's knowledge. I sensed he thought I would be upset that he no longer had the book. But I told him that if she was going to steal something, what better thing to steal? We laughed and agreed this was a "good" kind of theft.

Samantha began reading it every morning. Eventually she admitted that God was talking to her through this little book. His reach is like ripples in a pond. Eventually they become so large you can't see them, but you know they're still there. I am thankful when God allows me to see a few of the ripples of His life in others.

As I learned that Samantha's earthly life had ended, I recalled the first day I met Gabe, my prayer with Samantha, going to select a Bible for him and giving him the *God Calling* devotional when I knew he couldn't read English. I thought of the friendship I've developed with his sister, Celia, of being in the hospital when she delivered her new baby. I felt intense pain while Gabe cried over Samantha's life—but most important, I felt great relief when he told me she accepted Christ the day before she died. So many ripples.

I was scared that Samantha's death would take Gabe away from the Lord. I was afraid he would be mad at God. I was sick with the thought that he might not want to live anymore.

Why? I asked the Lord.

Even with all of my appointments, all of the examples, all of the proof, sometimes I doubt. I used to believe the people of the Old Testament were crazy, even idiotic, because they doubted God even after they saw all of His miracles. Now I know they were just like me.

When Gabe had received the call from Samantha's parents, they told him she'd prayed with them that Sunday and asked the Lord to be her Savior. They told him the *God Calling* book remained on her nightstand and she read it faithfully every day. She had called out for God's forgiveness on Sunday—and He took her home with Him on Monday.

I can't help but reflect on the words God spoke through me to Gabe that tense day in my car. I told him there were people only *he* could touch, and satan was scared of the man he would become in Christ!

I want you to know that Gabe is stronger today than ever. He teaches me so much about the power of Jesus. He told me that maybe God saved His life so he could help save Samantha's life.

"Yes, Gabe," I replied. "God knew she was going to die, and I believe He sent you on a God Appointment to bring her to Him. He trusted you with her life."

Then he said something I will never forget.

"Yes, Bobbie," he said. "Just like He trusted you with my life." The student had become my teacher.

Don't ever underestimate the importance of your Decision Point. One decision can bring eternal life.

11 Books, 11 Years

There is always a reason!

I recently arrived home from work completely excited to have the evening all to myself. The house was peaceful—no TV, no music, no ringing phones. I made myself a quick salad and considered reading a book.

About the time I settled down to relax, I received a call from my friend Theresa. Her car was at the mechanic's and she needed a ride to pick it up. Her son, Nicholas, could take her, but I felt called to give her a ride.

Theresa told me she'd printed eleven copies of *God Appointments*. The book wasn't published yet, but we wanted to give out some copies. For some reason that day, she decided to order eleven copies. As I dropped her off, she handed me the box of books. Once again I was excited to head home.

Driving through my neighborhood, I took a different route. Sitting on a neighbor's porch was a young girl. She had long, sandy hair with highlights from the sun. Her eyes were light blue; her face was like an angel's. Though she was fifty feet away, it was like I could see her close up. I waved. Our eyes connected and we both smiled.

Just minutes before, I couldn't wait to be home alone. Now that I was finally home, I could not shut the garage door behind me.

I jumped out of the car and walked toward the little blonde angel. I whispered, "I know this is you, God."

I said "hello" and asked how she was doing. She told me her name was Haley.

"Haley," I said softly. "I believe God wanted me to come over and talk with you."

Haley looked into my eyes. I had her full attention. It was a beautiful experience as I told her about God's love. I told her about the *God Appointments* book and how He can do amazing things through us when we are available to him. Just then her grandparents joined us, and we shared a wonderful conversation about life and the Lord. As I prepared to leave and walk home, Haley piped up.

"May I have one of your books?" she asked.

I was not expecting that. Up to that point, I'd only given the book to adults. I asked her grandparents if she could walk with me to my house to pick up a book. As we walked together I asked, "Miss Haley, how old are you?"

"Eleven," she said.

Eleven books. Eleven years. I couldn't stop smiling.

The moment Haley and I got inside my house, our conversation had no boundaries. She asked me question after question as we talked about some of the God Appointments described in the book. Each time I tried to hand her a copy, she'd ask me another question.

I assumed she had accepted Christ, but I had to make sure. I asked her if Jesus was her friend. She said "yes." I felt God telling me to ask if she had a Bible. She told me she'd lost her Bible when she moved.

When I'd bought Bibles to give to orphans in Africa, I'd picked up four extras. I already knew where three of them were going, but I kept the extra one in my car. Each time I opened the trunk I'd wonder, "Who is that Bible for?"

I was so excited to give that Bible to Haley — until I realized I was driving a rental while my car was at the body shop. *Not to worry*, I thought, *I'll drop by first thing in the morning to get the Bible for Haley*. I'd learned she was leaving her grandparents' home later that day, and I knew God wanted Haley to have this Bible.

My first stop the next morning was the body shop. I shouted something about an emergency and snatched the Bible out of my trunk. I raced back to Haley's grandparents' house. The moment I pulled up, she appeared at the front door. The beautiful blond angel had been waiting for me with her grandparents.

I told Haley how much I loved meeting her and that I hoped to see her again. We exchanged phone numbers and I asked her to contact me when she came back to visit.

Our conversation turned to *God Appointments* and the copy I'd given her the night before. Her grandmother told me Haley had stayed up late reading.

I couldn't believe how much she knew already as she quoted words from the book! God was up to something special, and I was blessed to be part of His plans for this delightful young girl's life.

Later I reflected on my encounter with Haley. I was excited to see how God continually gives me energy to do His work. The mere moment He gave me this appointment, I forgot about myself and what I thought were my needs to be alone and have time to my "self."

Haley did call me after she returned home. She wanted to share with me something she had never told anyone before. Haley told me she was now aware that she has a special gift given to her from God.

I'm thankful that God trusted me to help her understand how to use it for the Lord. I look forward to many special moments with Haley. God took an evening I thought I wanted and turned it into a night that I needed. I love when God trumps my life.

Chapter 19

Two by Two

When I think of each of my God Appointments, I realize that most of the time they are "two by two." It takes two listeners for every relationship and two listeners for every appointment.

My friend Theresa is a great listener. More than once she's called to tell me something, but I start talking before she gets to it. Only at the end of the conversation does she share her news.

"Hey," I say. "Why didn't you tell me that first?"

She instinctively says, "I wanted to listen to all the things that happened to you today."

Another friend of mine explains it this way: "It is better to be interested than to be interesting."

Theresa is always interested in what others have to say. Very seldom does she ask for help. Some people find our friendship peculiar because we come from very different backgrounds and on the surface we seem unlike. One difference is she's Catholic and I'm not. The two of us don't recognize this as a "difference" because what we have in common is way bigger! Jesus is always the third strand in our friendship. For He said, *"Where two or three come together in my name, there I am with them."*

The love of Jesus allows us to love and respect each others' differences. When I visit Theresa's church, she uses holy water to make the sign of the cross on me. Though I am not familiar with her church's traditions, I'm thankful she loves me enough to bless me. When she comes to my church, she wrinkles her nose at the lack of tradition, and I tell her to relax. Our differences never outweigh our love for each other, which comes from a common love of Christ. When we make our priority Jesus, it's easy for us to listen, learn and love.

This God Appointment began on a Saturday morning after I talked on the phone with Theresa. She mentioned that her church's food pantry was seriously short on help, and she worried about being able to take care of everyone who needed meals and support. I was listening to my friend ask for help in her nonintrusive way — yet I wasn't really listening.

In retrospect, I don't think she was really asking *me* for help. My old thoughts — spurred on by what this world teaches us — kicked in and overpowered what God would call me to do. It didn't even occur to me to offer my help.

The decision point came later that day. I asked myself, *Why didn't I offer to help? I'm not doing anything today.*

I'm ashamed to admit that part of the reason I didn't reach out is because I am not Catholic. In my spirit I knew it made no difference to Jesus or Theresa, but in my flesh I was filled with old thoughts.

The enemy makes a living by keeping God's people divided in Christ. This division is a lie straight from satan, because it's not possible for Jesus Himself to be divided. So satan picked the next best thing to divide — the church, aka God's people — and the whole world has fallen for it. That included me on this particular day!

Satan's next push was to plant seeds of disappointment in me. Remember: If the enemy can keep us focused on our mistakes, mess-ups, missteps and oversights, he can also keep us from doing what is revealed to us through the Holy Spirit. Never make your *wrong* more important than God's *right*.

What I needed was tough love from God — and that's just what I received. It went something like this: "Hey girl, get over yourself! There is no time for self-pity, and your friend needs help. Now go!"

We all fall down. But what do we choose to do when we get back up? We can walk away in God's strength, or we can stay and examine where, why and how we fell. If God doesn't stick around to measure the fall, why should we?

When I arrived at the food pantry, Theresa smiled at me. Without exchanging any words, I knew she understood everything I'd gone through.

Theresa and I have more than a friendship, we have Jesus.

Theresa always looks after me. One time she asked me to share my mission experiences with the junior high girls at her church. As I was speaking, a woman who was present questioned my thoughts and interpretations. Theresa bolted to the front of the class, her Bible in hand. She knows the Scripture better than I and wasn't going to let anyone throw a stone at me.

She found a job at the food pantry she knew I could do. My task was to put bread in bags. The orders came in quickly, and as I worked I thanked Jesus over and over for trusting and sending me to do His work.

One order came with verbal instructions: "Pack this order light because she is walking." I imagined the woman receiving these groceries, struggling to carry the bags home in nearly 100-degree heat. Theresa immediately went to check out the situation.

The recipient was a single woman, and the food pantry volunteers suspected she was homeless. I told Theresa I'd be glad to take her where she needed to go. We packed her bags extra heavy and offered her a ride. She said she was going to the library, but resisted my offer to drive her there. I could tell by her posture that this was not her regular routine. With more urging, she reluctantly accepted.

We were both uncomfortable on the drive. I attempted some small talk, telling her it was far too hot to walk. She said she would've been fine.

Looking down at the floor, she noticed part of my *God Appointments* manuscripts and asked about it. I explained that I was working on a book, a miracle in itself. She picked it up and held the pages. Her next statement surprised me.

"I went to college for publishing and worked in this field for years," she said.

"Tell me. I am listening!" I said.

She told me her husband had left her and she'd suffered a nervous breakdown. She hadn't been well enough to work for several years. She led the conversation back to my book, sharing with me the steps I could take to get it published. She encouraged me to write a synopsis and told me exactly how to do it.

I couldn't believe what I was hearing. The homeless lady at the food pantry was teaching me how to move toward publishing my book! Clearly she was sent by God.

As I dropped her off at the library, I opened my wallet and gave her all the money I had. I told her I was her God Appointment that day and thanked her for allowing God to care for me through her. With a strange expression, she asked if she could keep the printed copy of my book.

I wrote my cell phone number on the manuscript and asked to give me a call after she read it. Again I asked if she needed a place to stay. She was firm when she insisted that she did not. And I knew God had a place for her because He had a place in her.

On the return trip to the food pantry, I prayed in the spirit. I didn't have words to tell God of my love for Him. Jesus found a home that day in a homeless woman. I found a home that day because I chose Jesus over division.

At the pantry I relayed the story to Theresa. She smiled as she always does and said, "I knew something was going to happen." We continued our food pantry work united in Christ. *This moment gave God's breath away.*

That night at home I wrote an amazing synopsis for *God Appointments.* Several days later, my first package went out to a publisher—synopsis and all. I never question my God Appointments, yet God continues to give me more answers than I will ever deserve.

Several weeks later, I was driving to a lunch appointment while talking on the phone with my sister, Lisa. I recapped my story about encountering the homeless woman and sending out the publishing package. As we were wrapping up our conversation, I spotted the homeless lady crossing the road.

"It's the homeless lady!" I shouted to Lisa as I tossed aside my phone.

I pulled off the road, beeped my horn and yelled out the window.

"Remember me?" I shouted.

"I've been reading your book," she said. "It is amazing."

"I wrote the synopsis just like you told me," I told her.

It's hard to describe the look on her face at my words, the sheer sweetness of her expression.

I asked if I could give her a ride. She declined but promised to call when she had extra minutes for her cell phone. Through our brief conversation, she didn't break her steady stride, and before I knew it she was across the road.

I picked up my cell phone. Lisa was still on the line.

"Can you believe what just happened?"

We marveled over the beautiful fact that she showed up just as I recounted the details to my sister.

"Lisa, this is my life!" I laughed.

If the truth be known, my life is quite ordinary to God! When we release Jesus to love His people through us, however, the most extraordinary things result. He will help us laugh, cry, love, hope and, most of all, fall in love with His life in you and me!

In God's mission field, there's an expression called "new normal." When you return from a mission trip, your life is forever changed and you discover a new way of defining "normal." Let this life of love in Christ be our new normal!

Chapter 20

Nana Gone Nuts

J ust when you think you're on top of the world, the world can move. In this God Appointment, the world made me move in a way that was very...worldly. As you know from this book, I am open to learning about God and listening for His direction. Ours is a God of communication, and writing this book has reinforced that notion in a mighty way.

A really good friend of mine has vivid dreams and can interpret what God is communicating within a dream. Because of the dreams' significance and how they come to pass, I know God is behind them. I myself don't dream often, but the ones I do have are memorable and real.

I guess I was aware that God communicates through dreams, but I've never been all that interested until now. In the Bible, God communicated many times through dreams, and people like my friend receive knowledge through dreams. Maybe that hadn't happened to me because I didn't understand the language of dreams.

Our church was hosting a Bible study on dreams and encouraging us to be aware of dreams as a communication tool from God. Now, there is nothing more precious to me than listening to the Lord, so when I heard that God uses another delivery system, I was all ears.

Can you imagine if you planted a seed in the ground and then commanded it to grow? That sounds crazy and illogical, but that's what we do to God's people. We plant one seed in their life and expect them to make a decision to commit their life to Jesus and grow in Christ. Our work on earth will never be about the number of people we personally bring to Jesus. Rather, our job is to keep planting seeds, working in the fields and trusting God to yield His harvest. In other words, we shouldn't be looking for *decisions*, we should be looking for *disciples*.

After the first few Bible study sessions, I went to sleep each night anticipating my big dream. But nothing happened — not even a glimmer of a Divine Dream. It became comical, because each time I showed up at class I'd say, "No dreams!" Yet I wasn't the least bit worried that I was missing out. God knows I need more seed time than the average person.

Class didn't meet over the Fourth of July holiday, and the pressure to "dream a little dream" lifted. In fact, I forgot all about dreaming and discovered more God Appointments.

One morning I woke up dwelling on a dream I didn't want. It was about my grandson, Andreas. Or was it?

In the dream people were shooting arrows at my grandson and me, and one hit Andreas right in the head. I pulled out the arrow as he yelled, "Nana, I am fine!" And he *was* fine — no blood, no wound, no pain. Even so, I turned around and ran after the shooter. I was like a cheetah chasing its prey! I caught and tackled our attacker...and that's when I woke up.

I didn't understand the dream and certainly didn't want to tell anyone. I was terrified by the thought of someone hurting Andreas. So the next Monday at class I said, "No dreams!"

I listened as others explained that some dreams can seem bad and not from God, and felt prompted to pray over the situation. It was a wakeup call, reminding me of our immense power over every wrong occurrence on earth through prayer. I got my confidence back and found peace in prayer. I am learning my confidence is not found in a plan or a dream. My confidence needs to come from God's power over all things.

That Wednesday, I spent the evening with my grandkids. My friend's daughter, Rachel, joined us for dinner. Rachel wanted to start a Bible study for young people, and I trying to encourage her and be a good mentor.

After dinner, my grandson Andreas took off on his bicycle. A moment later, he passed in front of the window like a flash, ran into the house, flung himself on the couch and stared at the door.

"Nana," he said. "Some teenage boys just told me to get the f —- out of here!"

In the next second I was out of my seat, ready to go after the boys like a cheetah chasing its prey!

Andreas yelled, "No, Nana, please don't go!"

I ordered him to get in the car so we could find the offenders. But he refused to join me in my mission. His five-year-old sister, Lenox, was game.

"Nana, let's go get 'em!" she shouted.

Rachel volunteered to stay behind with Andreas. (Did she think this display was part of our mentoring program?)

Lenox and I took off like soldiers engaging in combat. We squealed around a corner, our eyes seeking the teenagers. I pulled into the alley and spotted them in a backyard nearby.

As I jumped out of the car, Lenox said, "Nana, don't leave me."

I grabbed her out of her booster seat and at the same time hollered, "You two! Over here NOW!"

One of the boys was mowing the lawn. He stopped, and the two walked toward us. Their expressions indicated they thought I was a crazy woman. (I'm laughing as I write this because I do feel out of control sometimes.)

"You'd better hope you are not the boys who cussed at my nine-year-old grandson," I admonished.

One of the boys spoke up rudely, telling me that Andreas had said he could mow the grass better than they could. I glared and said, "He is nine years old. Give me a break."

I prepared to unleash more of my harsh thoughts when the younger boy captured my complete attention.

"Ma'am, we did swear at him because he is really annoying. But I was wrong and I am sorry," he meekly said.

In one second, I went from firing from both barrels to total disarmament. This young gentleman, Andy, brought me back to a place of peace. In the next instant, I reached out and introduced myself. I told the boy I was proud of his response and said he was an example to me.

Looking at Lenox I said, "Did you see how Andy said he was sorry? He was a good example for us because Nana hasn't been behaving very well."

This was a teaching moment for me and for my grandchildren. I was so concerned with protecting the kids from the teenagers, and now this teenager had protected my grandchildren from me. We're never too old to learn—and we're even more blessed when young people do the teaching. I told Andy he had behaved in a Christ-like way and I was thankful for his life. I shook his hand, told him I was sorry and said that Andreas would be back to apologize as well.

I laughed at myself on the drive home, wondering once again why God chose me to write this book. It's true that He can tame anyone—even a wild Nana cheetah.

After I told Rachel the details, she giggled and said, "Let's go, Andreas. We need to apologize."

I didn't connect this episode to my arrow dream until I began to journal later. I'd originally thought the dream was about someone trying to hurt Andreas and had been prompted to pray. I believe the prayer prompting is true, but God has since revealed two things in common between the dream and the moment. Neither instance had anything to do with Andreas; he was fine both times. Rather, the experience had everything to do with me defending and protecting my position.

I believe God is preparing me for future attacks. Yet He gently lets me know that I don't need to defend myself or Him. Remember, Jesus did not even defend Himself as He was persecuted and crucified. His Father in heaven came to rescue our Savior in due time. Today we all are rescued in faith through Jesus! As I recalled the day, *this moment gave God's breath away.*

Going forward, I will *try* not to act like a cheetah. But if for some reason you catch me chasing prey, please pray and forgive me. I am just a Nana trying to love God's people.

Rachel, Andreas, me and Lenox… just another day in paradise.

Chapter 21

Life or Death?

I don't know much about death, and God is still teaching me about life.

Just the other day I received a text message from my brother, Shawn. He was telling me about a friend that had passed away and gave me the location and time of the funeral. I did not know his friend personally, but I know the man's brother and sister-in-law, Jeff and Julie. I made a note to send a card later.

The next morning I left town for a sales seminar, which just happened to be in the same city as the funeral—three hours away. But sometimes our minds don't make the connection God is giving us. We get distracted by our lives and miss hearing His voice.

Just after the seminar, my company was hosting a cookout—at the same time as the viewing. I'd already dismissed going to the viewing through logic and felt good about my decision. I enjoyed the cookout and talking with coworkers.

I happened to glance at my cell phone to check the time, and the viewing came to mind. I figured that if I left within five minutes, I'd have forty-five minutes to attend the viewing. I made the decision to go and quietly slipped away from the company gathering.

Why do I feel such an urgency to go? I wondered. I was tired, for one. And no one was expecting me at the funeral home.

By the time I reached the funeral home, I determined that God wanted me to say hello to Jeff and Julie—so I thought. I saw no one I knew as I moved to the casket, closing my eyes and praying for this gentleman's life.

I then moved toward a chair in the corner, passing a girl. She looked to be about twelve years old and was staring at me. I watched as she weaved in and out of the crowd. Her eyes were on me, so I waved for her to join me.

She sat down right next to me.

"I know you," she announced.

"Honey, I don't think so, because I don't live around here."

"I *know* that I know you," she insisted. "I just can't remember how."

Her eyes looked directly into mine, and I felt a connection with her. Her next words explained everything.

"I know you, but I don't know who you are. Who are you?"

God was with me, I knew then. I could feel His Spirit coming through me. I said that I believed God had sent me and asked her name.

She introduced herself as Scout. I told her I loved her name and I knew she was special. Our conversation was amazing, purely designed by the Holy Spirit, who gave Scout every-thing He wanted her to have. Soon another young person appeared—Scout's older sister, Zibby.

"Who are you?" she asked.

"Her name is Bobbie and God sent her to us," Scout explained.

Zibby was holding her rosary. As she looked into my eyes, I once again found the connection. The three of us talked about God and how He made us. The girls were full of ques-tions, and I felt like I was in heaven. I was no longer tired from my long day and felt the strength that only comes from God. Zibby had a friend with her, a young girl who was pregnant. I shared my own story about being a young mother. I told them about how Billie Lou came to be, and they listened carefully to each and every word. I sensed God wanted to love this young girl and give her words of lasting encouragement.

Before long, another young girl sat on the floor beside us. Her name was Scarlett, another sister. "Who are you?" she asked.

"Her name is Bobbie and God sent her here to talk with us," Zibby explained.

Scarlett looked into my eyes, and I could hardly reign in my emotions. My eyes welled with tears as she looked at me.

"Is that true?" she asked.

"Scarlett, there is no other place in the world I would rather be," I said.

By this time I had joined the girls on the floor. The funeral home was packed with people. As I shared the words God put on my heart, I felt a love far greater than my life here on earth. I recognized it to be the love, joy and peace that only the Holy Spirit can bring!

People outside our circle were staring at us. I'm sure they wondered who I was and why all these girls were clustered around me. Due to the intensity of our conversation, we paid no attention to the activity and chatter going on around us.

Just then I noticed a woman walking our way. She did not look happy.

"Who are you, and what are you talking to my girls about?"

"Your girls are beautiful, and you have done a wonderful job with them," I began. "My name is Bobbie, and I've been sharing how God made them and how much God loves them."

"Okay, thank you!" she said. Her tone and demeanor softened and she walked away, leaving us to our conversation.

"Don't mind her," Zibby said. "She's going through a lot and is taking this very hard."

The girls explained that the man in the casket was their mom's husband, their stepfather. He had been like their real father and they would sorely miss him.

There I was, sitting on the floor with the daughters of the man lying in the casket knowing in faith that God himself had sent me. It takes total faith to belief that He would trust any individual person to be His hands and feet. God is the special one; He flows out of us when we show up.

I shuddered to think I might have missed this privilege if I hadn't known God's voice. Many times I go without knowing why. But faith in God allows me to comfortably live on a no-need-to-know basis.

God protects us from using logic to deliver His plan. Logic, after all, is based on the things we can see. It's the opposite of faith. With each God Appointment, I grow stronger in faith — and you will, too.

The girls' mother returned to announce that she was ready to go, and I hugged each of them goodbye. Tears fell from our eyes. I asked them to take good care of their mother. At their request, we exchanged numbers and shared a warm group hug. I didn't want to let them go!

Even as I write this journal, I feel my heart wrapped around these precious girls of God. He has a plan for their lives and will bring people to help them grow. At times the hardest thing is to let His people go. I had to let go of the moment in my flesh and cherish it in the treasure box of my heart.

Just as the girls were leaving, I spotted Jeff and Julie. Julie said she'd noticed me on the floor but didn't want to interrupt because the girls had been listening so intently. Julie and I are friends and hadn't seen each other in many years, so I knew only God had kept her still so the girls and I could talk.

I turned my full attention to Jeff and Julie. We shared stories of the past and I talked with their kids, who had grown into beautiful young adults. This time with my old friends was just as special as my time with the girls. After all, we are all valuable to God.

Let's bring our lives to Him by showing up — and He will bring His life and love through us!

As long as God gives me life, I will "go" to give God's life to others — and I urge you to do the same. As in this appointment, He brings life in the midst of death! God's life in us gives His *breath* away.

Chapter 22

Beach Light

The Christmas holiday was coming to an end and I was preparing for my trip home. For the first time I'd spent Christmas in Florida with just my mom I and had enjoyed each moment. I told my mom I was going for a quick walk on the beach and suggested that we go to breakfast afterward.

Strolling from my mom's condo to the windy beach nearby, I remembered the many times I had followed this very path with my dad.

My habit was to walk toward the left pier. My dad had always walked left, and I had continued doing so after his death. On instinct, I repeated the pattern. I'm comfortable going along with tradition.

The morning was quite chilly, and I realized that if I walked toward the right pier instead, I would be able to feel the sun on my face for the majority of my walk. It made perfect sense—so why did I feel I'd be doing something *wrong* if I turned and walked in a different direction? I had never done it that way before....

Today, alone with my choice, I felt led to switch directions from the past. I confirmed the decision by welcoming the sun's warmth. Moving at last, I started to giggle uncontrollably.

Crazy? Perhaps. But there was such freedom in this seemingly simple decision!

I was so excited I broke into an all-out run. The experience was beautiful. I had my headphones on with worship music serenading me and God's beach beneath my feet. I opened myself up to pray in the Spirit.

Many times I pray in the Spirit by choice, but this day was different. Praying was as natural and easy as breathing.

Even as I worshipped and adored God, I realized how out of shape I'd become—and went from my spirit back to my body in less than a second. I stopped running, caught my breath and gazed out at the wide-open ocean. God gives us such beauty, and I am overwhelmed by His love.

I made it to the second pier and turned around, feeling great joy in taking this new route. On the walk back, I noticed another woman walking alone on the beach. I couldn't take my eyes off of her. She was adorable, with soft, curly gray hair and a purposeful walk. I felt the familiar nudge at my heart: "Tell her."

She too was wearing headphones, and I didn't want to bother her. But the nudge came a second time: "Tell her."

This was a Decision Point. I turned toward the woman and removed my headphones. Even before I spoke, she had removed hers too. The moment I met her eyes, I knew God had sent her.

"Hi," I said with the gentle boldness God gives me in these situations. "I just wanted to tell you that you are adorable."

She raised her hands to the sky and said, "Thank you, Jesus!"

"He is the one who wanted me to tell you that," I replied.

I told her about my decision to try a new route and emphasized that God's timing is perfect. I shared that I believed God wanted the two of us to meet. She confirmed our meeting had not happened by chance.

Her name was Loy. With tears in her eyes, she told me how that she had lost her son six weeks ago. She had been doing well, but this particular morning had been extremely difficult. I listened to her story, and we exchanged love and tears.

Was the appointment for me or for her? I have decided it was for both of us. What amazes me most about her story is the way she praised God. Even in the deepest, harshest pain of losing a child, she praised God for her son's life.

"When God planted Ricky in my womb, He did not promise how long I would have him," she said.

Again she raised her hands to the Lord and said, "I am so thankful that I had him for awhile."

I thanked this lovely woman — this grieving yet joyous mother — for taking time to teach me about God's love. She said I was an angel who reminded her how valuable she is to God. We hugged and, as often happens, I didn't want to let her go.

Back at the condo, I got another direction from God: "Give her your manuscript."

How would I find her again? I knew only her first name.

My friend Diane called then, and we talked for about twenty minutes. By that point I was justifying that there was no way I'd find Loy on the beach again. I lingered on my bed and looked over at my manuscript. I knew what I had to do.

This was a Decision Point. In faith I wrote Loy a note and put my cell number on the manuscript. I prayed, "Lord, if you want her to have this book, you will have to find her for me."

This time as I entered the beach, God led me to the left — the way my father always took me. The sun was bright, and I'd left my sunglasses in my room. Way down the beach, I saw a tiny silhouette that looked like Loy. I laughed and cried at once. I kept my eyes upon her as we moved closer.

"Lord, can this be true? It *is* her, Lord, and we are going to meet in the same place as before."

We were still too far away for words, but I could tell Loy recognized me. She gave me the sweetest wave of her hand. We both walked faster until we met, and we hugged once again.

Loy said she was praying for me and thanking God. I told her about the manuscript and how God organized our meeting place—the exact same spot as before. Only God could do such a thing.

This time it was even harder to part, but I knew it was enough.

At the condo, my mom was ready to leave for breakfast. We went across the street to the Sweet Sage restaurant.

My phone rang with a local call. The moment I heard her voice, I knew the caller was Loy. She told me she was sitting by the pool and couldn't put down the manuscript. She told me the current page number and recited the story.

"Bobbie, you were lying in bed looking at the ceiling, and the Lord put on your heart 'Life After Sin,'" she said. "Your next thought was, 'What do those initials stand for? L-A-S.' And then the Lord gave you the word Testimonies. Life After Sin Testimonies is the name of your ministry, right?"

"Yes," I said. "L.A.S.T. Ministries.

"My initials are L.A.S.T.!" Loy said, "Loy Ann Stottler Talbot."

She'd been reading the words in the manuscript, struggling to believe all that was happening. God was letting her know in a tangible way that her life would be alright. *This moment gave God's breath away.*

I thanked Loy for loving God and sharing His love with me.

With each appointment, God teaches me the value of mentoring. Today I was mentored by a woman named Loy. She was a light on the beach who brought me joy!

—

A special note: This God Appointment occurred on December 28, 2010. *God Appointments* was complete and ready to be published. I received this text message from my friend, Pastor Tavio, on January 1, 2011: "Did you add any more chapters to your book that I have not read? I was asking because I felt like the Lord was saying that you were to be led by Him to add something."

On January 2, I prayed, "Lord, lead me." I thought about Loy as I went to bed that night. On January 3, I woke up and prayed in the Spirit; within minutes Loy's initials came to mind: L-A-S-T. This journal came through me that day as it is written above. I am learning that each day is a new day to hear the voice of God! Thank you, Loy and Tavio, for your faithfulness.

Chapter 23

More than Enough in Chicago

Girls weekend in Chicago! We had more than enough food, more than enough clothes and more than enough cold and wind.

The twenty-five women in our group met Saturday morning for an hour of encouragement, and then we were ready, set, shop! Each of us had our own agenda.

This year was different for me. While I might normally splurge and indulge myself, I was in the middle of publishing *God Appointments* and was watching every penny. I had to make sure I had enough.

Oh, and did I mention I was holding tight to my money?

After our early-morning gathering, we separated into groups and hit the streets of the Windy City. I enjoyed the company of my friends without feeling the pressure to buy something. I made it in and out of several stores with all of my cash in my wallet.

As we walked to the next store, I could barely stand the cold and wind. My face was numb and breathing had become painful. To my right I noticed a woman and two children sitting on a crate.

One child was about nine years old; the other, wrapped in blankets, was lying flat on the woman's lap. I tried not to notice the details and even entertained thoughts like, *Those probably aren't her children and she's just staging to make money.*

I tried to pull my glance away but met eyes with the younger child. His eyes were familiar. The next voice in my head said, "Go back!" I felt relieved to hear God's direction.

I told the girls I'd be right back. Tricia and Patti knew without words where I was going, and each handed me an offering. I reached into my own wallet and said, "I know, Lord."

Again, this day was different. Normally I would hand over the money and say, "God bless you." Today I knelt down to say hello and tell the family I believed the Lord had told me to check on them. The boy sitting next to his mom wouldn't look at me, and the little one said, "You smell like powder."

I smiled and looked into his eyes once again. God has used these eyes to confirm His presence many times in the past.

The woman said, "Ma'am, I am not homeless. I'm short on my rent."

"Oh good," I said. "I'm thankful you are not homeless. Thank you for trusting me with the truth."

I explained that I used to be a single mom and at times I needed a little help. She asked how I got out of it. I told her that while I'm still not out of it, I'm learning to be thankful in it.

"I have different struggles now," I explained. "I may look all put together, but we are the same. We need each other! Please don't judge me for the way I look, and I won't judge you. God put us together and we are a perfect for Him. Just like today. I am grateful God is here to help us with our struggles."

I was compelled to confess.

"I want you to know I had bad thoughts as I walked by you the first time," I said.

The boy who wouldn't look at me glanced over and finally spoke.

"What were your bad thoughts, ma'am?"

I told him that my thoughts said the two of them probably were not her kids. In the sweetest voice, he said, "She *is* our mama."

It was a beautiful moment to share how we are made of body, soul and spirit. I shared how each day the enemy tries to put his bad image on us in the form of negative thoughts. I urged the boy not to listen to those bad thoughts and to be proud of his mother because of the way she loves him.

I went on to say that the Holy Spirit can give him direction—just like the direction I received to come back and speak to his family. It was a Decision Point to listen to Jesus over the enemy. He looked at me with a smile and laid his head on his mom's shoulder.

The youngest boy asked that I pray for them, and his pure request brought tears to his mother's eyes. I was overwhelmed with God's love and all the rest of Chicago was silent. As we bowed our heads, the Lord gave His *breath* away. I put my arms around them and gave much more than money could ever buy. I gave them the love God gave me to give.

I slipped the money into the mother's hand and kissed her tenderly on the cheek. As we touched our tears became one.

I tucked myself away between tall buildings as I wept and thanked God. In times like this I have to seek refuge to pray in the Spirit. I had more of God to release in thankfulness. I had to worship and praise Him in His language.

As I regained composure, I was ready to rejoin my friends and continue with the day. I let them know I had delivered their gifts and all was well. There was no way to explain what had happened, at least not right then.

The chilly day came to an end and our group returned to our hotel. There in the lobby was an ATM, and immediately I thought of the mother, struggling to provide for two boys and short on her rent.

"Lord, could they still be there?"

I asked Patti to start the coffee pot in our room and said I'd be right back. At the ATM, I retrieved the amount God put on my heart. That would allow me to help the woman and still keep back forty dollars for myself, to cover any necessary tips and provide a little cash for the trip home. That would be fine, I thought, because I'd be giving enough.

Back out in the bitter cold I prayed, *Lord if she is there, I will know this is you.*

I rounded the corner—and there they were. Walking faster I called out, "Hello!"

The next words I heard confirmed Jesus sent me there. The little boy cried, "You came back!"

This comment resonated because the children I visit in Africa always ask, "Are you coming back?" If you asked if they'd rather you send them money or come back, one hundred percent of the time they say, "Please come back!"

This cold night on the streets of Chicago I said, "Yes, honey. I came back."

I looked into the woman's eyes and asked, "How did you do? Have you made any more money?" With thankfulness she said, "About seven more dollars."

I let her know the Lord sent me back and slipped the additional money into her hand. She didn't look at it but her tears told me everything. I asked what it would take for her to be able to go home and get out of the cold. "Around one hundred dollars," she sighed.

Now she looked down at the bills in her hand and saw a twenty dollar bill. The money was folded so she could see only the bill on the outside. She let out a scream and said, "That is enough! That is enough." She was crying and jumping, and the boys were smiling.

The next moment gave God's breath away.

"Give her more than enough" came to my mind.

I told her God wanted her to have more than enough. Following God's direction, I opened my wallet to give her the forty dollars I was keeping back for the trip home. She moaned and dropped toward me, collapsing in my arms. Our spirits became one as we exchanged pain, tears, joy, hope and most of all love.

The three of them walked away toward home, and the older boy looked back at me and waved. Once again my heart felt separate from my body. The pain was sharp as a knife.

I had found love in Chicago—and love will always be more than enough. But sometimes love can be incredibly painful.

I just finished reading the book *Dangerous Surrender* by Kay Warren. Her words describe the pain that occurs when the heart feels separate from the body. Kay belongs to what she calls the Seriously Disturbed and Gloriously Ruined Club. Being part of this group means saying "yes" to God, knowing this decision leads us into uncomfortable—even painful—places.

I've joined the ranks of this club—and it's worth dying for, if you ask me. I am thankful for people like Kay and for my new friends in Chicago. To me they represent the women, men and children who will do "whatever it takes."

Reflecting on this God Appointment, I see how this nearly homeless mother possessed an honesty and humility—and that released a willingness inside me to give. She never asked me for money. I believe God wanted her to have much more than money. My work in missions has taught me that it's as important to be involved in someone's life as it is to offer money.

I wonder now if the boy asked me about my bad thoughts because he was ashamed for being outside on the streets with his mother. I see that God used our bad thoughts to give us a connection point.

I'd held back forty dollars with good intentions, yet God gently reminded me that He always provides. And He gave me more than enough when he confirmed His presence through the child who cried, "You came back!"

The Holy Spirit guides us back...see you soon.

Chapter 24

Never Goodbye

In the beginning chapters I shared many of the treasures God has given me. I'm still amazed at how He designed us to complement each other, and how we are made in His image. As such, our relationships with one another should mirror our relationship with God.

I also shared how the enemy can influence our mind/soul and body. I'm not telling you I have it all figured out now, because I struggle with my mind and body as much as the next person. God gently reminds me each day I have no right to judge or measure anyone else.

I want you to know if I mess up along the way, please do not blame God for my failings. He has nothing to do with my bad choices. He has everything to do with the hope I have for our lives as brothers and sisters in Christ. Something good always comes out of God's Kingdom through relationships when we allow the Lord to be involved.

We often need to be reminded to see others through the eyes of God. He chooses to see the good in us; we must choose to see the good in others. I believe God wants us to exercise our mind in the Holy Spirit to make it strong and confident. God's people have years of built-up wounds. We use these wounds as a protection, almost like a shield, to keep any more pain from getting in. The enemy has complete awareness of this tactic, because he developed it. It keeps him tangled in our lives and keeps the focus on ourselves and away from the very thing that can set us free. If we aren't aware of our *spirit*, the only thing we rely on is our mind and body. This explains why many of us are held captive by the enemy with addictions, depression and pain.

Don't be too hard on yourself. One of the last thing Jesus said before he died on the cross was, "Father, forgive them, they do not know." I thank God for what I do know. Jesus died so we would know how much His Father loves us. He came back to give us the Holy Spirit. We are children of the Almighty, and we have complete freedom from the enemy. I have to work on this every day because the enemy tells me I can be bought for a price. As I renew my mind in God's Word I'm reminded I am not for sale. I belong to the One I was created for and nothing on earth compares.

Jesus came so we may be worthy and willing for His Father. We have a choice to believe the lies of satan or to choose Jesus and accept the gift He left for us in the Spirit. When we let Jesus love God's people through us, we bare the image of who we were created to be. This alone will bring us love, joy, peace, patience, kindness, goodness, faithfulness, gentleness and self-control.

God also gives us a special language the enemy cannot understand. The work we have here on earth is to prepare our hearts, our lives, our peace and our ability to let Him love His people through us. Do not wait to be better, stronger, smarter or even more spiritual. Each time we have a God Appointment, we allow Jesus to work through us and in that process we become more than enough. God gets all of the glory, because He does all of the work. We just have to be willing to listen to his voice.

In the "Nothing New" chapter, you read 1 Corinthians 2, and then I encouraged you to read it again at the end of the book. I hope you do this with new eyes to see the Spirit and heart of God.

In closing, let me say that it's never "goodbye," my friends. I hope to see you here on earth, but if not here then surely in Heaven. I want to hear about your God Appointments on www.GodAppointments.com. Wear your God Appointment Break (GAB) bracelet with love. When you see someone wearing a bracelet, use it as an invitation to ask about their God Appointment. Go GAB!

Writing this book has been the greatest privilege of my life. That you would take the time to read it allowed me to give God's *breath* away! It allowed me to give God *breath* away! Job 33:4 says it best, *"The Spirit of God has made me; the breath of the Almighty gives me life."*

One more thing.... Please read through the God Appointment Break study guide in the back of this book. It can help you host GAB gatherings for many generations to come!

Finally, I'm thankful to my Aunt Delores for mentoring me and sharing her relationship with Jesus. She imitated Him, and that made me want what she had. She gently showed me the way, and now I am blessed to show you how to accept God's free gift of forgiveness and the power of the Holy Spirit.

To understand why and how God's gift is free, take a look at these verses:

- Romans 3:23
- Ephesians 2:1-4, 5-10
- Romans 6:23
- 1 John 1:9
- John 1:12
- Romans 10:9-10
- Luke 19:10

If you haven't already accepted the gift of salvation and the Holy Spirit, remember it is there for you. You simply have to accept it.

If you have accepted this gift of salvation but want to renew your life through awareness of the Holy Spirit, you can start with a simple prayer like this one:

"Lord Jesus, I believe you are the Son of God. Thank you for dying on the cross for my sins. Please forgive my sins and give me the gift of eternal life. I ask you into my life and heart to be my Lord and Savior. Lord, help me better serve you through the baptism of the Holy Spirit. May I use your gifts to bring honor to your name, Jesus. Amen."

Now it's time to say "thank you" to Jehovah God with each day of our lives. Together we are privileged to serve Jesus and His Father with our God Appointments.

Thank you!

*G*OD *A*PPOINTMENT *B*REAK
Go *GAB!*

Gatherings for churches, small groups and friends

GAB gatherings are a wonderful way to build bridges within the church, in small groups and between friends. A certain discipline comes from being available to pray each morning, to listen and to release the direction of the Holy Spirit.

In *GAB* gatherings, we can share:

- **Faith** that God will send us.
- **Trust** that God will give us the words.
- **Belief** that the Holy Spirit transforms lives.

Each God Appointment begins with a simple prayer, so let go and release God to do the rest.

Guidelines for *GAB* gatherings

Open each *GAB* gathering with prayer, and then review the points described below. Together, you can prepare the environment in which your hearts can give and receive.

WARNING: Do not measure your appointments. Each appointment belongs to God and is designed for His glory.

IMPORTANT: Please do not forget to journal your God Appointments! Hidden treasures are revealed as we give away our words to paper. We give because we have and so that others may receive.

CRITICAL: Come as you are! I wrote this book just as I am. God did not say, "Bobbie, get your life in order first." He was more like, "Bobbie, as you step out in faith to write this book and love My people, you will find My order." Please come just as you are! You are more than enough.

CAUTION: Be careful when sharing thoughts not to speak negatively about other churches, organizations or God's people. Jesus reminds us to forgive people because they do not know. Each *GAB* gathering should be a safe place and a no-negativity zone. You can share personal struggles that relate to the study guide questions. Please bring solutions that will unite us, not divide us, in Christ.

Suggestions for *GAB* gatherings

- **Churches**
  Share a God Appointment in the church bulletin or allow individuals to share their God Appointment with the congregation. Encourage small groups to hold *GAB* gatherings.

- **Small groups**
  Review the "Thoughts to consider" in the study guide that follows and let the Holy Spirit guide you. Encourage group members to share Bible verses that reveal additional understanding.

  ☐ Review *GAB* gathering guidelines at the start of each meeting.

  ☐ Use the "Thoughts to consider" section as your *GAB* gatherings study guide. It is divided to accommodate your study time for each gathering.

  ☐ Allow time for each person to choose a God Appointment from the book and give a short overview of how it impacted his or her life.

  ☐ When individuals are ready, encourage them to share God Appointments from their personal journals. A blank journal is located in the back of this book.

  ☐ *GAB* gathering host and guests: If you are pleased with your gathering experience after completion, consider hosting your own gathering. Send an invitation to several people with directions to come with a copy of *God Appointments*. Set a date for your first gathering and let people know they can read as they go.

  Optional: As a host you can order *GAB* bracelets to present as your guests share their first personal God Appointment. You can also direct them to the website to get bracelets on their own.

- **Friends**
  Create an environment where you expect the best from each other. Ask someone to be your *GAB* accountability partner. Be accountable to read your Bible daily, pray in the Spirit, listen…and go *GAB!*

- *God Appointment* **books and merchandise are available at** <u>www.GodAppointments.com</u> or 1-855-GAB-1212 (1-855-422-1212). *GAB* bracelets are a wonderful way to share God's love, and they serve as a simple reminder of your God Appointments. You will also find journals, t-shirts and additional *GAB* merchandise. Let's give them something to *GAB* about!

GOD APPOINTMENT BREAK Special thanks to my friend, David Endres for the inspired creation of the GAB logo and artwork.

God Appointments Study Guide
Thoughts to Consider

GAB Gathering I

A. Why do you think Bobbie cites 1 Corinthians 2 to demonstrate the wisdom of the Holy Spirit? How do you think she relates to Paul in writing this book? (See pages xii -xiii.)

_____

_____

_____

_____

_____

_____

_____

B. Do you think *experience* is important? How does God use our good and bad experiences to connect us with His people? Please share an experience that has helped you give grace and forgiveness to another person. (See page 13-14.)

_____

_____

_____

_____

_____

_____

_____

C. What has satan accomplished by covering the Holy Spirit from us? Which two areas of our body, soul/mind and spirit can be influenced by satan? Why? (See pages 18.)

_____

_____

_____

_____

_____

_____

_____

D. How can our lives be limited here on earth when we accept only a portion of what Jesus died for? (See pages 21.)

_____

_____

_____

_____

_____

_____

_____

$\mathcal{GAB}$ **Gathering II**

A. When we celebrate the success of others, how are we taught to appreciate the growth of God's Kingdom? Give examples of your successes and failures, and describe how each made you feel. (See page 22.)

_____

_____

_____

_____

_____

_____

_____

_____

B. What's the difference between proactive and reactive God Appointments? Do you think both can be good for God's people? Which type should we make a priority? (See page 23.)

_____

_____

_____

_____

_____

_____

_____

C. What does it mean when people say, "When Jesus died we received the garden back"? Is the Holy Spirit the connection that satan took away in the garden? Why did God make a language that satan cannot understand? (See page 24-25.)

_____

_____

_____

_____

_____

_____

_____

_____

D. Does it grieve God when we don't understand His language? Why or why not? Give an example of a time you tried to reach out to someone and that person denied your love. (See page 26-27.)

_____

_____

_____

_____

_____

_____

_____

_____

$\mathcal{GAB}$ **Gathering III**

A. Do we have everything we need to fight the battle against satan? How do we release the power we have? (See page 26.)

_____

_____

_____

_____

_____

_____

_____

B. How does praying in the Spirit compare to breathing, eating or making love? Can we intercede for another human being, or can each of the above only be experienced by the person executing the act? (That is, can we breathe for someone else?) (See page 29-30.)

_____

_____

_____

_____

_____

_____

_____

C. Did Jesus build the church on Peter the man or on the thought Peter had through revelation about who Jesus was? Can we know things from God through the Holy Spirit if we believe and have understanding like Peter? Share something you believe came in a thought from God. (See page 30.)

_____

_____

_____

_____

_____

_____

_____

D. Does your soul/mind or body change when you accept Jesus as your savior? Why is it necessary to spend the rest of your life renewing your mind? How can satan stop you from understanding what you have here on earth? (See page 30-31.)

_____

_____

_____

_____

_____

_____

_____

GAB Gathering IV

A. How strong could a relationship between you and another person be if you don't spend time with him or her? How much stronger can it be when you communicate your deepest thoughts and feelings? How is knowing *of* Jesus different from knowing him intimately? (See page 35-36.)

_____

_____

_____

_____

_____

_____

_____

_____

B. Do you think Paul had a healthy viewpoint of the private language of God? Was his opinion selfish, or was he obedient to God's directed order? Have you ever been turned off by religion that was delivered from a person? If yes, give an example. Was this experience directed by God or man? (See page 37.)

_____

_____

_____

_____

_____

_____

_____

_____

C. Why do you think Bobbie believed she could write this book without any experience or knowledge on her own? What gave her the courage to follow God's calling? (See page 38.)

_____

_____

_____

_____

_____

_____

_____

D. Why do you think God gave Bobbie one thought or revelation at a time? How does this compare to the direction God gave Joseph? Share a personal example of a thought or revelation you have received from God. (See pages 43.)

_____

_____

_____

_____

_____

_____

_____

$\mathcal{GAB}$ **Gathering V**

A. How did God use people in Bobbie's life to deliver His plan? What did they bring to the party, and how did they complement her? What people in your life were used by God to deliver something bigger than yourself? Describe that experience. (See pages 44-45.)

_____

_____

_____

_____

_____

_____

_____

_____

B. Why do you think Bobbie shares how she came to know the Lord and offers guidance in taking that step? Share your personal story of how you were introduced to Jesus, including your reaction to that invitation. (See page 189-190.)

_____

_____

_____

_____

_____

_____

_____

_____

C. Why was it difficult for Paul to describe the forgiveness of sin? How does this compare to today's culture? What part of us — body, soul/mind and spirit — asks, "If our sins are forgiven, why don't we just go out and sin?" (See page 5-6.)

_____

_____

_____

_____

_____

_____

_____

D. Does God hate our sins (i.e., our mistakes and mess-ups), or does He hate what those sins can do in our lives? If you feel comfortable, explain how a sin has affected your life in a certain area. How you can use your experience to bring love to others? (See page 7.)

_____

_____

_____

_____

_____

_____

_____

GAB Gathering VI

A. Why does sin make us turn away from God? How does God teach us that He never turns away from us? Describe examples of this from your own life. (See page 7.)

_____

_____

_____

_____

_____

_____

_____

B. How can God's love make us holier accidently than we try to be on our own? How does the law or legalism strengthen sin? (See page 8.)

_____

_____

_____

_____

_____

_____

_____

C. As a group, discuss how God is pouring out His Spirit. How we could mistake God's Spirit for satan's spirit if we don't understand the language of the Holy Spirit? Satan's spirit always comes to kill and destroy. God's Spirit gives life! Give examples of people you know who have experienced the counterfeit spirit. (See page 8-9.)

_____

_____

_____

_____

_____

_____

_____

_____

D. How have the *GAB* gatherings helped you trust what you believe? Share an example of how you or someone you know has experienced transformation from the Holy Spirit.

_____

_____

_____

_____

_____

_____

_____

Additional GAB journals can be purchased at www.godappointments.com or 1-855-GAB-1212 (1-855-GAB-422-1212).

Personal *GAB* Journal

Date

Personal *GAB* Journal

Date

Gift Collection

In a world where the norm is to keep your head down and not become involved in situations with people you don't know, Bobbie's life and her beautiful stories are a vivid reminder to me that some events and encounters happen by God's providence. I'm learning through her that paying attention to others and listening for direction from God can cause amazing change for others — and also for me.
Jane Williams
Former Corporate Vice President

Without a doubt God Appointments *is a page turner. I could not wait to find out what Bobbie would encounter next and which way God would lead her. She expresses her experiences with people all over the world, with God guiding her every inch of the way. Because Bobbie wrote this book, I have a new way of seeing just how God can use us when we learn how to pray in the Spirit and decide once and for all that without Him we just simply exist.*
Diane Keelan
Business Owner

God Appointments *has changed my life and my relationship with God. This book really showed me the importance of prayer and the Holy Spirit at work. I feel very blessed!*
Jessica Ziegler
Hairstylist

In my first conversation with Bobbie, I found her to be a person who has goodness and kindness and trust in the Lord beyond imagination. She exemplifies Christian grace as she desires to bring attention to the workings of our Lord. Bobbie practices what she writes, and I pray her gracious spirit will shine through in this challenging book as she beautifully shows how God faithfully works under the radar.
Dr. Paul Risser
Author, *An Eye For Miracles***; Lifelong Pastor and Former Church President of the Foursquare Gospel**

Rarely can I sit and read a book cover to cover. After watching Bobbie's life unfold while applying what she has written, I was compelled to learn more. "The Gift" in Bobbie's life was always at work even if she was unable to put words to it. The love displayed to every human being this author encounters is a true testimony to the LOVE of Jesus Christ. It inspires me to love my husband and children without conditions. I count it a privilege and blessing to have sat at the feet of a woman who desires nothing more than to give "the gift" away again!

Valorie LeFevre
Home-School mom of two adorable children

Bobbie is an intensely devout lady who obviously desires to be an encouragement, inspiration and help to those who have a hunger for God and will take the time to read God Appointments.

Jesse Pitts
Retired Principal and School Board Member

Whenever Bobbie shares, I listen! Her life and this book demonstrate such an example of the Spirit working in her and through her. I love seeing God's hand in everything she shares! She speaks life into situations, and it is so refreshing to hear. I truly thirst for more. I love the expression "God Appointments," and it truly has opened my eyes and heart to see God at work and to see a willing servant respond to the call!

Karen Stromquist
Home-School Teacher

Bobbie serves our Creator on a daily basis and never questions His guidance. As her work in the mission field testifies, Bobbie is devoted to God's people. This book was written with the hand of the Spirit.

Jim Richardson
Business Owner and Philanthropist

Bobbie has a wonderful way of articulating her daily life with Jesus. What some might consider "radical" Bobbie lives out as normal, day-to-day experiences. It is refreshing to read her stories of daily Spirit-led adventure in these days of hyper-planned and programmed lives.

Doug Ehrgott
Missions Pastor

THERE IS SOMETHING DIFFERENT ABOUT THIS!
Joe Smith
Christian Sales

God Appointments is like a how-to book for finding a deeper relationship with God. It is powerfully moving and very difficult to put down. I just wish I could have had it when I was twelve. It is a book I will read over and over. I want to share it with all of the people I know, because it describes something everyone needs to understand as early in their lives as they can. For me, reading this book was like seeing what I need to do 'with glasses on' for the first time. I am lucky enough to know Bobbie personally. From the moment I met her, I knew she was someone I wanted to know better. At first I didn't know why, but the more you know her, the more apparent this feeling becomes. She exudes love for everyone, and it's fun to be around her just to watch the impact she has on everyone she meets. I didn't always understand that God was speaking through her, but it was clear to me how she deeply and sincerely cares about everyone she meets. Now I understand what attracted me to Bobbie – it's like having Jesus among us. I hope from reading this book to become a little more like Bobbie. I too can change the world through the ripple effect. God bless Bobbie and the faith she has to listen so we can learn.
Nancy Burton
Corporate Bank Manager

I thank Bobbie for sharing God Appointments *with me. She writes clearly and movingly and has significant material to work with! God is using her in unusual and sometimes dramatic ways in response to her faithfulness to the Spirit's voice. I am grateful she has brought her spiritual sensitivity to the work of Horizon International.*
Barry L. Callen
Author, *Hope on the Horizon;* **NPO Corporate Secretary**

You can see Jesus just shining through this woman! God has sent her to this earth to do His work. It is very apparent. She is not letting Him down.
Ann Hannan
Special Projects Coordinator

I was particularly moved by the story of Bobbie and her love for her father. It had me crying in public and really deepened my understanding of how great the Father's love is for His children!
Dawn Dunkman
Emergency Room Nurse

Bobbie's book is amazing! It made me cry, laugh, ache, trust and understand how to listen for the Holy Spirit's leading in my life. The 'thought or revelation' explanation totally opened my eyes and heart.
Nicole Levang
Mother of Four Young Boys

This book touched me in so many ways. I got tears in my eyes at the beginning of it. The stories made me smile and humbled me. There are family members and friends for whom I will buy this book as a gift. That's what it is: a gift.
Nancy Naber
Pharmaceutical Product Manager

Reading through the manuscript made me realize that God Appointments should be a normal part of the Christian life. The Holy Spirit makes these available to everyone. We should be making a difference every day in the world around us.
Pauline Murnane
Interior Designer

I wanted to share this story with you: I started reading God Appointments this morning, during my breakfast. I left the file open on my computer, and when I came back home my dad said, 'Audrey, how much have you read of that book? It's so great!' Soon he was printing off pages to underline and highlight and was looking up stuff on the computer. He's just so pumped. It's pretty cool how the Holy Spirit is working already. Bobbie's book offers such a fresh perspective on what it means to walk in the power of the Holy Spirit. The book left my family and me with many 'aha!' moments; it really helps us to learn what it means to live out our faith in Christ!
Audrey Witta
High School Student

God Appointments *is heart-warming. Bobbie is humble enough to share her journey with God. It's very inspiring to see God working in her life and the lives she touches. Anyone who wants to know they are not alone and their concerns are being heard should read* God Appointments.
Ellen Pichereau
Registered Nurse

WOW! I am so overwhelmed by this book. I laughed and cried. I was incredibly moved. When I read the chapter "God or Gun" I thought, What would I do? *When I read the chapter about Zimbabwe I thought,* What would I do? *But I guess I'm asking the wrong question. It's not about what* I *would do, but what God would call me to do or give me the words to speak. This book is going to touch so many people in so many places. Well done, faithful servant!*
Amy Ashcraft
Project Manager

God Appointments *has touched me like no other book today. It's rare when you just can't put a book down. You must keep reading to understand the treasures inside. Each page is written with love, kindness and compassion. The book warms your heart and soul and leaves you wanting more.*
Lisa Swims
Wife, Mother and Sister

God Appointments *has been such an awakening for me. Bobbie's walk in serving the Lord speaks such volumes. Reading the book and knowing Bobbie have taught me to be courageous about serving the Lord and speaking the truth to others. It also has changed my relationship with God. I am closer to Him now than I have ever been before. I have such a beautiful inner peace and joy now that are flowing onto my family and the people who surround me. I know that speaking in the Spirit has been the fuel to my growing relationship with God. The truth that is written in this book needs to be told! So many are afraid to express it for fear of what others will think. Praise God for sending His words through Bobbie!*
Andrea Holsworth
Wife and Mother

I just finished reading God Appointments.... *What can I say? I marveled my way through it. The stroke of Bobbie's pen was influenced by God and by her own heart. This book inspires me to get a journal and start recording thoughts, prayers and experiences. I know that Bobbie and I have come into each other's lives by the grace of God. Thanks to her, a little boy named Letabo is receiving our sponsorship in South Africa, "one life at a time." Bobbie inspires so many people, and I can honestly say she has inspired me, too. She is a valuable resource for reaching out to bring Light to a dark and hurting world.*

Francene Foster
Corporate Communications Manager

I know I did not meet Bobbie by accident. She has many unknown assigned appointments from God. She is definitely an instrument in God's hands. She is a beautiful example of God's hands and feet doing His work on earth.

Loy Ann Stottler Talbot (L.A.S.T.)
Widow, Mother, Grandmother and Friend (see "Beach Light")

Quite apparent by the end of page nine, I felt like an 'appointment' was made and kept, on my behalf, on a random flight to Indy — my first but not my last.

Thanks be to our Lord, Jesus Christ, in His name — and thanks to Bobbie.

Michael Stefanchik
Medical Intelligence